Titanic: The Truth On Trial

By

Ian Donaldson

Dedication

For my wife, Suzanne, who strives to keep me on an even keel.

Copyright

Copyright © 2023 Ian Donaldson All rights reserved.

The contents of this book, not freely available in the public domain, are subject to copyright restrictions, therefore, no parts of this book may be reproduced or copied in any form, or stored electronically within an off-line data retrieval system, or transmitted in any form or by any means, e.g., written, photographic, electronic, mechanical, photocopying, or any other means of reproduction or storage without the express written permission of the author/publisher.

The views and opinions expressed herein are those of the author.

ISBN-13: 9798390227244

ISBN-10: 1477123456

Cover design by: Ian Donaldson

Contents

Dedication

Copyright

Contents

Note

Foreword

Introduction

The Foundations of Fallacy

Who Breaks A Butterfly Upon A Wheel?

Yes Minister

And Finally?

"There be dragons..."

Epilogue

About The Author

Bibliography

Index

Note

We know discrepancies exist in the numbers of persons carried, lost, and saved on the Titanic. The British Inquiry reported that the total number of persons employed on board in all capacities was 885 men and 23 women. The total number of passengers was 1,316, totalling 2,201 persons on board. The number of those saved was 711, and the remainder, 1,490, died. While remaining respectful, avoiding confusion, and maintaining consistency, we will continue using those figures given in Lord Mersey's Report. Those adjustments made since then do not significantly alter their importance.

Foreword

On the day, the loss of the passenger steamship R.M.S. Titanic was confirmed at Lloyd's, the famous London-based insurance underwriters, as tradition required, the Lutine Bell was struck once. The peel of that bell, salvaged from another shipwreck decades earlier, might also have been heard across London through the corridors of the White Star Shipping Line and the Board of Trade offices in Whitehall, the beating heart of H.M. Government in the U.K., its doleful toll an unwelcome harbinger of recrimination, heralding much-needed reform.

"It is not merely of some importance but is of fundamental importance that justice should not only be done, but should manifestly and undoubtedly be seen to be done."

(Lord Hewart, Lord Chief Justice of England; *Rex v. Sussex Justices,* [1924] 1 KB 256.)

Introduction

"Whoever digs a pit will fall into it, and a stone will come back on him who starts it rolling."

(Proverbs 26:27)

During the Wreck Commissioners Inquiry into the loss of the Titanic, prominent witnesses testified before Lord Mersey in defence of the collective decisions made in the preceding decades by various Government committees and officials. Without providing credible evidence to support their assertions, they insisted that for twenty-odd years before the Titanic sank, safe practices and rigorous design were instrumental in policymaking and proven by comparatively incident-free Trans-Atlantic shipping passage, which justified their wise decisions and sound reasoning. However, the shipping casualties documented by another source, Lloyd's Shipping Register, for the same period are inconsistent with official Government figures revealed by these witnesses during the Inquiry. These records indicate many more passenger and cargo vessels coming to grief while attempting the North Atlantic passage and still more across the world's oceans and seas. One witness of long-standing government service, whose track record in manipulating numbers to suit his argument had previously been raised in Parliament. Across the

Atlantic, in the Washington offices of the U.S. Senate, those Senators who had roundly condemned what to them appeared to be the effete members of the Board of Trade, whose "*laxity of regulation and hasty inspection the world is largely indebted for this awful fatality*" would likely view this shameful segment of the British Inquiry in the pejorative sense of a 'dog and pony show'. There would be no justice, biblical or otherwise, brought to bear on the heads of these Board of Trade civil servants or White Star executives. Nor was there to be public exposure of the deception on show, a revealing of the guilty perpetrators during the British Inquiry, or within the findings of Lord Mersey's Report.

The collective mendacity of these officials would remain unchallenged long after the official Inquiries delegates had packed away their fountain pens and ink pots, notepads, and briefcases. Evidence suggesting official malfeasance is contained within the Inquiry transcripts and contemporary documents that had existed from the beginning before the notional gavel came down on the Inquiry proceedings *sine die*. Until now, no Titanic researcher has unearthed the details of these witnesses duplicity in their narrative to bury the truth in the reams of official documents produced in evidence for the Court. The assumption was, of course, that the "*evidence which justified the Board of Trade*," as the Attorney-General, Sir Rufus Isaacs, mooted, was accurate. These influential officials were about to confound the issue with their own interpretation of the Board of Trade's statistics, produced for the Inquiry by the Marine Department. This manipulation of these figures suggests the Board of Trade mandarins, in cahoots with their legal briefs, resorted to presenting shipping casualties, creatively edited, and delivered with enough ambiguity to disguise their true meaning and support their strategy, which amounted to finding refuge from accusations of departmental lassitude. At the same time, preserving their lucrative careers, uphold their reputations and salve their consciences. During their time giving evidence, there could be some confusion, even today, over the questions and responses that can be inferred from the transcripts.

The details and significance of this part of the Inquiry have largely been forgotten or overlooked by historians and authors, presumably dismissed as irrelevant. However, viewed through the lens of objectivity, any attempt to disguise the actual numbers of shipping casualties and lives lost smacks of a different agenda; to prevent the Inquiry from getting at the truth. If this was indeed the case, then Lord Mersey was also being led along the same path to his eventual conclusions by being denied or dismissing the actual shipping figures. It is no exaggeration to state that the basis for Lord Mersey's conclusions were partially framed upon these questionable shipping figures and the supposed modest loss of life, recorded within. We know Lord Mersey used these spurious numbers to base his supposition that to steam ahead at top speed had been acceptable practice largely due to this "*immunity from lo*ss," ostensibly previously enjoyed by Trans-Atlantic passages. From there, it is but a short step to the exoneration of the White Star Line and E.J. Smith, captain of the Titanic. Many of those observers down through the years who have sought to find reasons to support the widely held belief that the outcome of the British Inquiry was a 'whitewash' need to look no further than the dubious presentation of the shipping figures for proof.

The Foundations of Fallacy

"Never let the truth get in the way of a good story."

(Unknown)

On the 18th day of the British Inquiry, Harold Sanderson, Vice-President of International Mercantile Marine, owners of the *Titanic*, was appearing before Lord Mersey. On this, the second day of his testimony there was one area in particular counsel for the White Star Line, Sir Robert Finlay, wanted to explore. During this part of his evidence, Sanderson was asked a series of questions with the likely intention of getting the responses recorded onto the Inquiries Minutes of Evidence. Under ordinary judicial proceedings, it would not be acceptable for counsel to introduce evidence or refer to statements during closing arguments that had not been raised during the formal hearings. Sir Robert Finlay opened this phase of his questioning;

> "Have you looked up the amount of loss of life in your vessels that has happened while your line has been running? - We have had some figures made up. Sanderson replied. Is this the statement? (*Handing same to Witness.*) - Yes, we prepared that statement. The statement goes from 1901 to 1911. - Yes."
> (Brit Inq 19732-3)

It is important to note that in his opening question, Sir Robert Finlay asked about the "*lo*ss *of life in your ve*ss*els*" and specified the period in question as "*while your line has been running,*" which would be from 1845, not the brief eleven-year period Sanderson was about to furnish. Also, Finlay had said "*your ve*ss*els,*" implying not losses exclusively from passenger vessels on the North Atlantic route to New York. White Star operated many ships that could also transport fare-paying passengers. As a skilled and experienced jurist, Sir Robert Finlay had to have had a strategy in mind from an early stage in which direction he desired the evidence to lead; the acquittal of all blame or responsibility for his clients, the White Star Line and Captain E.J. Smith; therefore, getting Harold Sanderson's figures on White Star losses onto the Inquiry notes was part of his objective at this point. The reason becoming clearer further on.

As this was a Wreck Commissioners Inquiry and not a criminal trial, there was no jury to deliberate on the evidence against the accused as there was no one in the dock facing prosecution. There were limited sanctions that could be brought to bear, typically, if a ship's officer were found to be blameworthy, this commonly entailed suspension of their certificate for a period decided by the Commissioner.
(See Captain Williams, Atlantic 1873 below)

Meanwhile, Sir Robert Finlay went on;

"The statement goes from 1901 to 1911? - Yes. Taking the result, apart from the loss of life that took place on the "Titanic" up to that time, how many passengers during those 10 years had been carried, and what was the total loss of life? - The total number of passengers shown by these figures carried during those 10 years is 2,179,594; the loss of life is two."

Finlay continued;

"When did that happen? - That happened in the case of the "Republic," which came into collision with the "Florida," and those two people were injured in the collision. - That was in January 1909? - Yes, that is right. I think these were first-class passengers? - They were. And is that the whole amount of loss of life which took place in that number of passengers carried? - Yes, it is."

The Commissioner interjected;

"How many passengers do you say you have carried in those 10 years? - The 10 years in question - 2,179,594," Sanderson replied.

The Attorney-General: "Is it not eleven years? 1901 to 1911 - both inclusive?"

The Witness: "I expect it is inclusive; in fact, it must be. You are right; it is eleven years inclusive."

Sir Robert Finlay continued;

"Adding the figures of the "Titanic" to that, and taking the loss of life, what is the total number of passengers carried and the total loss of life, and what percentage does that yield? - Including the

"*Titanic,*" the total becomes 2,180,910 passengers and loss of life 822. The percentage is 038."
"I will hand that statement in." (The statement was handed in.)
(Brit Inq 19734-42.)

Significantly, there is no further reference to the statement mentioned in the Final Report.

The figure of 822 includes only passengers who lost their lives. Of the 673 officers and crew, no acknowledgement or salutation was offered by Sanderson in commemoration of their sacrifice.
(Authors note; according to the Wreck Commissioners Report the loss of life, was 673 crew and 817 passengers, making a total of 1490.)

It is the significance of the responses which disarms the Court to the imprecision in the form of the questions and the likelihood that this testimony and the responses had been carefully rehearsed. We can be pretty sure Harold Sanderson did not calculate the loss of life in his head as a percentage while in the witness stand. Sir Robert Finlay would have appreciated in advance the neutralising effect of such a seemingly low figure on the Court.

Sanderson was also tactlessly playing down the fact that 6 people died as a result of that collision, 3 crewmen from the *Florida* and 3 passengers from the *Republic*. One, the husband of one of the other victims, would later succumb to his injuries in hospital. Sanderson was only including those White Star passengers who were killed at the time of the collision and not the crewmen from the *Florida* or any others who were mortally injured.

These fatalities were known to the White Star Line and, incidentally, the Board of Trade, but the White Star Line chose to interpret the figures differently, more favourably to their argument. The lives of the crewmen, at least as far as Harold Sanderson was concerned, apparently, did not count. During his final summations, Sir Robert Finlay would state;

> "*How can it be said that there was something wrong with a system which yields such a result as that?*" (Authors Italics)

These subtle manipulations formed part of the corporate 'cleansing process' of exonerating White Star from culpability. The numbers, however low, of those who died were not corrected by the Attorney-General, who was, of course, according to the Prime Minister, acting "*solely in the interests of the public.*" Yet he corrected Sir Robert Finlay's error of arguably less significance; "*Is it not eleven years? 1901 to 1911 - both inclusive?*"

The exact circumstances surrounding the collision between the *Republic* and the *Florida* were shrouded in mystery. The incident occurred during the Board of Trade Presidency of Winston Churchill and should have given rise to an official investigation. That there was no public record of there being any formal inquiry into the circumstances of the collision, in dense fog, with the loss of life remains a mystery wrapped in Board of Trade 'officialese'.

In the process, Winston Churchill apparently decided to bypass his obligations under the articles of the Merchant Shipping Act of 1894. Neither the White Star Line nor Lloyd Italiano, operators of the Florida presumably, would have been pressing for an Inquiry, in either case, running the risk of shouldering the blame for the loss and any pecuniary damages resulting.

Fresh from his successes as Under-Secretary of State in the Colonial Office, in April 1908, Winston Churchill was promoted to President of the Board of Trade, at the age of 33, the youngest member of the Cabinet since 1866. If anyone at the time believed that Churchill might bring his reputed progressive thinking to his new role, they would have been disappointed.

He may have harboured a belief that his political fortunes had improved beyond measure, but he had, in fact joined a Government department immersed in political and Parliamentary apathy.

His predecessors were mere caretakers of a stifled organisation that would stand accused of Ministerial complacency and industrial nepotism, particularly towards ship owners. Regrettably, his reputation for drive and energy was not to be directed towards outdated Merchant Shipping regulations. Churchill was not about to put his reputation or career on hold. It is not wrong to harbour the belief his own political ambitions went above and beyond the welfare of seamen or the rules that governed the safety of vessels at sea.

In Parliament however, when Sunderland M.P. Thomas Summerbell asked the reason;

"Why there has been no public inquiry into the wreck of the S.S. "Republic" early this year?"

Mr Tenant the Parliamentary Secretary to The Board of Trade replied;

"The "Republic" sank after collision with the Italian steamer "Florida" in American waters on 23rd January last. Formal investigation was not ordered in this country, as the Board of Trade had no power to compel the attendance of witnesses from the Italian vessel, and any public inquiry that might have been held in their absence would necessarily have been of an *ex parte* character and possibly prejudicial to the interests of the English vessel. Actions were entered in the United States District Court, and are, I am informed, still pending. It was reported in the newspapers that the "Florida" had been arrested by a United States marshal and subsequently sold by auction."

(Wreck of Steamship "Republic" (Inquiry). HC Deb 30 June 1909 vol 7 cc379-80)

A representative of the Government quoting an article from a newspaper as substantiation in the 'Mother of Parliaments', is disrespectful and defies belief. The outcome of the legal action remains unknown. A contemporary source reported that the *Florida* was purchased by another Italian-owned shipping line, Ligure Brasiliana in 1911 and renamed "*Cavour*."

(theshipslist.com)

In his questioning of Harold Sanderson, Sir Robert Finlay was purposely focusing exclusively on White Star passenger vessels and, characteristically for the period, seemingly, only first-class passengers who were killed at the time of the event and not those who might have succumbed later.

Upon his (Sanderson's) death in 1932, the New York Times reported his obituary;

"He was appointed first vice president of the I. M. M. in 1902. He had also been on the boards, in many cases as chairman, of Shaw, Savill & Albion, Ltd.; Atlantic Transport Company, Ltd.; Frederick Leyland & Co., Ltd.; International Navigation Company, Ltd., (Red Star and American) and other shipping companies."
(The New York Times, February 26, 1932.)

Sanderson's business interests exceeded solely White Star Line vessels. Similarly, during his own testimony before the U.S. Senate Inquiry, Philip Franklin Sanderson's counterpart in the United States, was asked;

"What composes the International Mercantile Marine Co.? Mr Franklin. In a general way, the International Mercantile Marine Co., through its various ramifications, owns the White Star Line, the American Line, the Red Star Line, the Atlantic Transport Line, and the National Line, and the majority of the stock of the Leyland Line."
(U.S. Senate Inquiry Day 3)

Entire shipping lines were regularly subsumed commercially, into larger competitor's fleets. Individual vessels were chartered, bought, and sold. Names were changed, even in defiance of the age-old sailor's superstition of renaming a vessel bringing bad luck; as Long John Silver said, "*Now, what a ship was christened, so let her stay, I says.*"
(Treasure Island)

Keeping track of vessels various comings and goings over time became an onerous task. Records get lost, details forgotten, and ships and their histories faded into obscurity. A great many vessels came down the slipways of yards in Belfast and Glasgow, on Tyneside and the Mersey. Ships of all descriptions and sizes. All would be constructed to similar exacting specifications and regulations. Shipbuilding in the UK at the turn of the 20th century was a colossal enterprise, employing a vast workforce. On completion, they steamed off decorated and painted in the customer's livery destined for ports in Europe to the Americas, the Far East, and the Antipodes. A century and more after Nelson's famous victory at Trafalgar, British ships and shipbuilding did indeed rule the waves.

Mercantile Marine tonnage owned by the four chief Maritime Powers:-

	Ships	Tonnage
British Empire	11,495	19,012.294
United States	3,469	5,098.678
Germany	2,718	4,833,186
France	1,465	1,882.280

(The Wreck Register and Chart. August 1912. Volume: 21 Issue: 245)

"*Corporations have neither bodies to be punished, nor souls to be condemned; they therefore do as they like.*"

(Edward Thurlow, 1st Baron Thurlow. 1731-1806. As quoted in John Poynder, Literary Extracts (1844), vol. 1, p. 268).

The above quote was said to have been made during the heady days of Georgian Colonial expansion and was, many believe, in reference to arguably the world's first truly multinational corporation, the (*in*)famous East India Company.

Indeed, the company could have been a template for every other avaricious conglomerate that came after and was reputedly engaged in aggressive business practices that are familiar today, conquering markets, eliminating competition, securing cheap sources of raw materials, protecting supply, and developing political alliances. Also, in keeping with the time, probably not without a fair sprinkling of bribery and corruption of government officials thrown in for good measure.

Projecting forward to the first decade of the next century and substituting the East India Company for J.P. Morgan's International Mercantile Marine and you have a similar scenario with I.M.M.'s reputed global aspirations of dominating the world's shipping lines.
J.P. Morgan's I.M.M. owned a vast fleet of vessels operating across the world's oceans and, as such, were exposed to the same perils of navigating treacherous stretches of water in the pursuit of trade and profit as their competitors. Ships went missing, ran aground or foundered in bad weather and heavy seas. Passengers and crews were lost, and families mourned their passing.
Harold Sanderson and Philip Franklin's positions as respective vice-presidents of I.M.M. harboured a corporate interest in many shipping lines. Any prospective acquisition of a rival firm would entail due diligence in the desired shipping lines operating costs, profits, and losses when they occurred and were known before I.M.M. assimilated them into the fold. Whatever the cause, past shipping casualties would be included as part of that process. These losses

were known to the owner's representatives during questioning before the U.S. and British Inquiries. Some examples might include the following;
On February 6, 1881, the Leyland Lines S.S. *Bohemian*, a subsidiary of I.M.M. since 1902, was wrecked off Mizen Head when she ran aground when bound from Boston for Liverpool with a cargo of bacon, cotton, and silk. 35 of the 57 crew were lost.
(Dictionary of Disasters at Sea During the Age of Steam: 1824-1962, Vol 1 A-L. Charles Hocking, 1969)
Three years later, on May 15, 1884, another Leyland Line vessel, S.S. *Illyrian*, the sister ship of the *Bohemian*, bound from Liverpool to Boston, was wrecked when she went onto the rocks near Cape Clear lighthouse. Her crew consisted of sixty-eight men, and mercifully, on this occasion, all were saved.
On November 21, 1885, another Leyland vessel, the steamship S.S. *Iberian* bound from Boston to Liverpool, was wrecked on the south coast of Ireland. Again, fortunately, there was no loss of life. Sadly, the same could not be said of the National Lines S.S. *Erin*, which was reported missing following her departure from New York on December 31, 1889, heading for London. There were 72 souls on board. In July 1890, a tragedy of a different kind befell a National Lines vessel, the S.S. *Egypt*, on route from New York to Liverpool, which caught fire and was abandoned; although there was no loss of life, her cargo could not be saved.
(norwayheritage.com)
In 1896 Atlantic Transport Line took over the fleet and assets of the National Line. Although ATL was an American company, it was effectively operated as British.

ATL itself was subsumed into the International Mercantile Marine Company in 1904.

In January 1895, the S.S. *Venetian* of Leyland Lines from Boston to London was wrecked on the aptly named Spectacle Island. Although she had accommodation for passengers on this occasion, she carried only cattle and general cargo. There were no lives lost.

November 15, 1898, saw the S.S. *Londonian*, another Leyland Line vessel on route from Boston to London, capsized and sank mid-Atlantic with the loss of 17 lives.

(Dictionary of Disasters at Sea During the Age of Steam: 1824-1962, Vol 1 A-L. Charles Hocking, 1969)

When the Atlantic Transport Lines S.S. *Mohegan* ran aground on the Manacles Rocks off the Lizard Peninsula on October 14 of the same year; 62 crewmen and 44 passengers out of a total of 143 onboard were lost. The Porthhoutock lifeboat saved those who survived. The sinking was described as, "*the greatest disaster in the history of the Atlantic Transport Line.*"

(Dictionary of Disasters at Sea During the Age of Steam: 1824-1962, Vol II M-Z. Charles Hocking, 1969)

The vessel, known then as the "*Cleopatra,*" had been originally ordered by the Wilson & Furness-Leyland Line. However, it was renamed "*Mohegan*" by the Atlantic Transport Company, who bought her while still on the slipway in a Tyneside shipbuilders' yard. On only her second voyage to America, disaster overcame her. Among the 106 who lost their lives, all the crew members perished, leaving no one who could explain what had happened on the ship. Hence, the tragedy was ascribed to human error.

Perhaps, they should have taken heed of Long John Silver's solemn portent.
(www.thevintagenews.com)

January 1899 saw the S.S. *Port Melbourne*, belonging to the National Line, reported missing on a voyage from New York to London; there were 52 souls on board.
(wrecksite.eu)

The same year saw the loss of the Dominion Lines S.S. *Scotsman,* bound from Liverpool to Montreal and was wrecked on Belle Isle with the loss of 13 lives. As usual, behind the grim statistics lay stories of human suffering. It was reported.

> *"In addition to the 11 known to have been drowned, at least 12 or 13 more afterwards perished from the exposure and hardships to which they were exposed on that terrible island at Belle Isle. And possible other casualties will follow, while many will be left with impaired constitutions."* (Authors Italics)

(The Bedford News. Friday, October 6, 1899)

The Dominion Line was acquired in 1902 by I.M.M. It was in the best interests of the shipping lines that the survivor's accounts of their experiences remained confined to the smallest readership. However, little escaped the Press, and the harrowing accounts of the sinking and subsequent allegations made the front pages of the New York Times.
(New York Times, Oct 1, 1899)

In 1902 when the I.M.M. Company was formed, the shares of the Dominion Line were among those acquired.

The year 1901 saw the Leyland Line's sixth loss since 1881 when S.S. Assyrian came to grief, wrecked off Cape Race, without loss of life.

At the commencement of her Atlantic voyage, S.S. *Waesland* of the American Line was lost on March 8, 1902, off Anglesey, North Wales, after colliding in fog with the S.S. *Harmonides* with the loss of 2 of the *Waesland's* passengers.
(New York Times, March 8, 1902.)
Very little is known about the exact fate of the 2119grt vessel, S.S. *Camorta*, a Clyde-built and British registered vessel carrying both cargo and passengers for the British India Steam Navigation Co. However, it is believed that she was struck by heavy seas on May 6, 1902, when crossing the Bay of Bengal in an area notorious for tropical cyclones called the Baragua Flats, just off the Irrawaddy Delta. Late in April 1902 she departed Madras bound for Rangoon in Burma with 655 passengers and 82 crew. She was due to arrive in Rangoon on the 6th of May. By the 13th May there was no sign of the *Camorta*, and she was reported as overdue.
Other British India vessels were dispatched to search for her. Initially a lifeboat was found near the Krishna lightvessel. The wreck was subsequently found by the S.S. *Purnea* on 4th June, lying in 15 fathoms of water with the top of her mainmast just showing above the water.
Although not an I.M.M. vessel, the S.S. *Camorta* was the fourth worst loss of life for a British registered vessel after the *Titanic*, *Lusitania*, and the *Empress of Ireland*.
(wrecksite.eu)
(Dictionary of Disasters at Sea During the Age of Steam: 1824-1962, Vol 1 A-L. Charles Hocking, 1969)
International Navigation Co., the parent company of the American Line, changed its name in 1902 to International

Mercantile Marine Co. and acquired the majority of shares of the White Star Line, Dominion, Atlantic Transport and Leyland Lines, as well as owning Red Star Line.
(www.theshipslist.com)

In his position, Harold Sanderson was in full knowledge of the losses, both human and cargo, sustained by I.M.M. shipping interests. For I.M.M. the losses were an inherent risk of the business they were in. Insurance of the vessel and its cargo softened the financial loss. A willing 'pool' of available crew could easily be found around the main UK shipping ports to replace those seamen that were lost.

Until 1914, in the years before the opening of the Panama Canal, vessels trading U.S. east coast to U.S. west coast ports faced the additional journey time and hazards of Cape Horn on the southernmost tip of Chile's Tierra del Fuego peninsula. Cape Horn was a place that gave mariners the aptly named 'heebie-jeebies'. The unpredictable, turbulent waters of this rocky promontory, where the Atlantic meets the Pacific, are particularly hazardous, owing to strong winds dubbed the 'Roaring Forties'. Giant waves, strong currents, and even occasional icebergs posed a 'perfect storm' of hazards to shipping.

On May 28, 1903, the clipper-ship *Aristides*, belonging to Aberdeen White Star, was reported missing on her voyage from Chile to San Francisco; 27 officers and crew were on board.
(Dictionary of Disasters at Sea During the Age of Steam: 1824-1962, Vol 1 A-L. Charles Hocking, 1969)

February 1904 saw the Red Star Line's S.S. *Conemaugh* from New York to Seattle believed lost in the vicinity of Cape Horn with 40 souls on board.

(www.maritimequest.com)
In June 1907, the former Leyland Lines S.S. *Nicaraguan* from Norfolk, Va. to Dublin was reported missing, with the loss of 50 crew continuing a dismal record of failure.
(www.wrecksite.eu)
Perhaps the Leyland Line is best remembered, surprisingly, not for losses at sea but for their most debased vessel, the S.S. *Californian*, which would play a prominent part in the unfolding saga of the *Titanic*. We already know that Sir Robert Finlay grudgingly acknowledged the loss of life aboard the S.S. *Republic* in January 1909. That same year, in August 1909, the Shaw-Savill vessel S.S. *Maori* was wrecked with the loss of 30 lives off Duiker Point on her way from Cape Town to New Zealand. Many of these vessels linked retrospectively with I.M.M. and in the boardroom at least, under the watchful eye of their grasping owner, J.P. Morgan.

Not a comprehensive list; for reasons explained previously, there will inevitably be omissions and inaccuracies. Nevertheless, in this brief account, the lives of an estimated 440 passengers and crew were lost in 16 incidents spanning three decades of I.M.M. associated shipping.

Given this involvement in such a vast mercantile empire, many with vessels familiar with the Trans-Atlantic passage, Sanderson was presenting the results purely from the perspective of the White Star Line, subtlety orchestrated by their wily counsel and only passenger vessels at that. Passengers alone need not lose their lives to illustrate that many sea voyages are often fraught with danger, as many ships' crews were lost at sea and scarcely warranted a mention.

In the eleven years alluded to by White Star counsel Sir Robert Finlay, across the oceans of the world, there were numerous notable cases involving vessels, many of whom we know were built in British shipyards and most of these also registered in Britain. This was two decades or so before the disparaging term 'flags of convenience' became a label associated as a means to circumvent maritime regulations. Sir Robert Finlay would later contest that the figure of "*only two lives*" lost on White Star vessels warranted risk-taking behaviour.

Had Sanderson responded to Sir Robert Finlay's original question, "*Have you looked up the amount of loss of life in your vessels that has happened while your line has been running?*" a different picture altogether would have emerged. The loss of the *Titanic* was not the first time the White Star Line found itself in the limelight of public scrutiny when a large passenger vessel was lost. As in many criminal trials, it is a legitimate practice to raise a witness's past felonious history as it often speaks to the credibility of any statements given in evidence. In Sanderson's case, the shipping record of the White Star Line pre-*Titanic*, is as informative as it is revealing.

In the early hours of April 1, 1873, the White Star passenger steamer S.S. *Atlantic* bound for New York with 957 passengers and crew, diverted to Halifax, miscalculated her position, and ran aground onto the rocky shores of Nova Scotia and was wrecked, resulting in the deaths of around 562 people. This included all the women on board and nearly all of the children The exact number was never established.

(www.ssatlantic.com)

The name *Atlantic*, it seems, was to prove to be a portentous choice of designation for a ship, as no less than five vessels of that name were to come to grief around the shores of Nova Scotia in the years leading up to the First World War.

The foundering of the *Atlantic* was to become the most significant loss of life in Nova Scotia's long history of shipwrecks, the second biggest in Canadian history, and until the sinking of the S.S. *La Bourgogne* on July 2, 1898, the largest marine disaster in the North Atlantic.

The fact that for modern-day recreational diving, Nova Scotia offers no less than 5,000 charted wreck locations tells us something of the difficulties ships had gotten into around the coastline over many years.

As they did in 1912, the New York Times in 1873 also led with accounts of the disaster that befell the *Atlantic*. Unlike the early stages of the *Titanic* story, using their vast network of resources, they were able to interview eyewitnesses on the spot to tell of the tragedy, from passengers and crew who survived the wreckage and in good time to circulate the story for the next day's early editions. Many early reports were met with disbelief and dismissed as the work of 'April Fool's Day' pranksters. It was only later that confirmation of the enormous loss of life began to emerge.

In scenes, similar to those which would take place almost 40 years later, when news of the loss of the *Titanic* became known, another White Star vessel was thrust onto the world stage when the Liverpool offices of the White Star line were besieged by the relatives and friends of those on board desperately seeking news of any survivors. As it would transpire, few would rejoice in their salvation.

The day before, on March 31, believing the *Atlantic* was running low on coal and unable to hoist sail due to the strong headwinds and fearing they might not make it to New York, Captain James Williams diverted to Halifax to take on more fuel. As it transpired, they had, in fact, more than enough remaining coal; the safety margin had been incorrect in what was to be among a series of poor decisions and failed communication. In heavy seas and strong winds, unfamiliar with the strong currents around the Bay of Fundy, Captain Williams believed the ship to be near Halifax, Nova Scotia, when it was, in fact, some 12 miles farther to the west, near the fishing village of Lower Prospect.

Had it not been for the selfless heroism and determination of the local people, the number of those who lost their lives would have been much greater. Local fishermen rallied soon after the news spread that the ship struck upon the rocks. Undeterred, they launched their boats to rescue survivors clinging to life on the wreckage of the crippled ship. Meanwhile, the local villagers unselfishly struggled to care for those that had managed to make it to shore.

In the aftermath of the sinking, there were reports of indiscipline among some of the crew during the voyage and in scenes that would be repeated when the *La Bourgogne* foundered, a desperate struggle for survival with sailors allegedly using force to get aboard the boats that had come out to rescue them. A court was convened to investigate the cause of the disaster, and the Report concluded that.

"The conduct of Captain Williams in the management of his ship during the 12 or 14 hours preceding the disaster, was so gravely at variance with what ought to have been the conduct of a man placed in his responsible position."

The captain was censured by suspending his certificate for two years for his conduct leading up to the disaster. Mr Brown, the fourth officer, was also censured for want of vigilance and violation of the captain's orders by suspending his certificate for three months. For many, the tame judgement passed on those whose "*want of vigilance*" contributed to hundreds of deaths only confirmed the belief that justice for the victims in shipping inquiries was low on the list of priorities.

(maritimemuseum.novascotia.ca / novascotia.ca)
(norwayheritage.com)

During the questioning of Harold Sanderson, counsel for the White Star Line may have wanted the Court to believe the losses column in White Star's record of Trans-Atlantic crossings to appear impressive; a closer examination of the company's overall safety record makes interesting reading. The reports and numbers suggest that passengers who boarded a White Star/I.M.M vessel in the decades preceding the *Titanic* disaster may have had more to fear from the questionable practices of her officers on the bridge than any storm at sea or chance encounter with an iceberg.

In 1910, the Panama Lines, S.S. *Finance*, on route to the Canal Zone with 85 passengers on board, sank off Sandy Hook on November 26, 1910, after being rammed by the White Star freighter S.S. *Georgic* in thick fog. Three passengers from the *Finance* and one crewman died in the ensuing panic. While Sanderson may have felt justified in his self-righteous testimony regarding the safety record, he boasted, his selective figures revealed only what he wanted the Court to hear. With a complicit counsel leading the line of questions and an indifferent audience in the Scottish Drill Hall, it was no wonder there were no serious efforts to probe deeper to expose any irregularities.

On February 11, 1893, the White Star passenger-cargo vessel S.S. *Naronic* departed Liverpool, bound for New York, carrying 77 persons on board. After dropping her pilot at Point Lynas, Anglesey, Wales, she was never heard from again.

(Dictionary of Disasters at Sea During the Age of Steam: 1824-1962, Vol II M-Z. Charles Hocking, 1969)
(www.whitestarhistory.com)
(New York Times, March 2, 1893)

By restricting his statement purely to the decade leading up to the *Titanic*, Sanderson, (or Finlay) was able to omit *Naronic* altogether from his testimony. No one in the Court commented, especially the representatives of the White Star Line, who would have recognised the deliberate omission in Sanderson's assertions. During his testimony, Harold Sanderson did not even pause for thought when one of his own company's vessels, its entire cargo, 74 officers and crewmen and 3 passengers went to sea in 1893 and never reached port. Despite Sir Robert Finlay's machinations to keep the *Naronic* out of the Inquiry records by only citing the period 1901-1911 in the figures he presented to the Court, *Naronic* would not escape scrutiny. The fate of the *Naronic* would resurface and become the subject of discussion towards the end of the British Inquiry when Sir Robert Finlay would attempt to discount the possibility that the *Naronic* came to grief by striking an iceberg. Counsel for the White Star Line would dismiss the disappearance of the *Naronic* as irrelevant, presumably because the 3 listed as passengers were not first-class passengers and similarly, the 17 cattlemen who were aboard when she departed. By including them in the ship's articles, they would have counted not as passengers but as crewmen. *Naronic* was not alone among Trans-Atlantic vessels to mysteriously vanish.

In the same period Harold Sanderson gave, 1901 to 1911, Lloyd's Register of Shipping for British and Foreign vessels records 62 British vessels reported as 'missing'. Over the same period worldwide, shipping losses due to being reported as 'missing' were recorded as 220. In every 'missing' category, the implication was the loss of life for all on board, the actual numbers unfortunately not recorded in Lloyd's records.

(For more information see: www.maritimearchives.co.uk. www.rmg.co.uk. hec.lrfoundation.org.uk)

Considering the Inquiry was tasked with ascertaining the causes which led to the loss of *Titanic* and lessons that could be learned, it is interesting to note that the Court accepted Sanderson's figures without question.

While Harold Sanderson may have taken some satisfaction from his claim that White Star vessels were untouched from such catastrophes that befell their rival shipping lines, their record for calamity was not, unimpeachable. It was in Sir Robert Finlay's interest to portray the White Star Line as exemplary in their Trans-Atlantic record. His presentation to the Court reflects these 'low' figures as testimony to sound navigation and prudent seamanship.

In what would herald the start of an inauspicious period of calamity on January 27, 1889, while approaching New York, White Star's S.S. *Republic* ran aground off Sandy Hook and was refloated five hours later. Whilst tied up in the dock, a boiler flue exploded, scalding ten crew members, three of them fatally. The *Republic's* Captain, a certain Edward J. Smith, reported only slight damage to the ship.

(The New York Times, January 28, 1889)

In 1907, the White Star Line came close to another disaster resulting from flawed navigation and excessive speed in poor conditions, a familiar theme. The S.S. *Suevic*, with 382 passengers and 141 crew and 12,000 tons of cargo, struck rocks off Lizard Point on the last stretch of her voyage from Adelaide to Liverpool. In scenes reminiscent of those from the Atlantic disaster decades previously, the dramatic rescue of the passengers and crew from the *Suevic* made headline news. Passengers and crew owed their lives to the heroism of the volunteer crews of the Cornish lifeboats. Sixty-odd members of four RNLI stations endured 16 hours of peril to bring the stricken victims ashore to safety and the welfare provided by local inhabitants who turned out in appalling conditions to assist them when they reached the shore. The incident came very close to an unmitigated disaster for all aboard. The subsequent rescue in 1907 set the record for the number of people saved in a single operation in the RNLI's brief history. This justifiably proud achievement still stands to the present day. The consequences for the White Star Line might otherwise have been even more dreadful.

(1907: The Suevic rescue - Timeline - Our history - RNLI)

On November 5, 1909, the New York Times reported that the S.S. *Adriatic*, again under the command of a certain Captain Smith, ran aground at the southern end of the Ambrose Channel at the entrance to New York harbour. There, she is stuck fast for five hours before a rising tide and tugboats were able to get her clear enough to continue. Near misses also do not seem to have perturbed the White Star Line when S.S. *Baltic* was involved in a collision, in fog, off Sandy Hook in July 1910 with a German oil tanker. First reports mentioned a *Baltic* crewman to have lost his life, presumed to have been thrown overboard during the force of the collision. However, later reports claimed that a seaman from the S.S. *Standard* had been injured and required hospital treatment. Bad luck or lousy seamanship seems to have plagued the White Star vessel *Baltic*. On March 13, 1907, in fog, the *Baltic* collided with an unnamed coal barge that sank off New Jersey. *Baltic* was undamaged and was able to continue. The vessel's propensity for calamity continued. On May 8, 1907, at the start of a voyage from New York, *Baltic* ran aground in the Swash Channel whilst supposedly avoiding a collision in fog and remained there until the next day when a high tide and guided by tugboats, she was able to continue her voyage. In a rather curious article on May 19, when the *Baltic* had safely docked in the U.K., passengers complained that the captain censored telegrams to exclude any reference to the grounding.

(New York Times, May 19, 1907)

As tenuous as White Star's relations with the Press were, a message embargo imposed by the Captain may have had something to do with the complement of wealthy and influential passengers, Andrew Carnegie, for example, and several other notable business executives.

It seemed wireless telegraphy was not only helpful in sending out signals of distress but also in averting distress in the stock exchange should word escape of an accident at sea to befall major financial players. Sceptics may prefer to say that any reason to restrict messages otherwise would be plain paranoia from an otherwise 'twitchy' White Star management.

Another report in the New York Times on November 23, 1907, told of the *Baltic,* this time under the command of Captain Ranson, where she was said to have run her bow onto the New Jersey shoreline. Witnesses from the nearby rescue station said it took nearly an hour for the vessel to drop anchor and reverse off. The next day, White Star officers denied the *Baltic* was the ship spotted. Nonetheless, the New York Times devoted a few column inches to the story.

(Baltic Bumps Jersey Shore. New York Times, November 23, 1907)

The White Star Line's run of bad luck surely could not last. However, the *Baltic* was again involved in another sea-going drama when, on January 23, 1909, in heavy fog off

Nantucket, The S.S. *Republic,* the same *Republic* mentioned earlier by Sanderson, was in a collision with the Lloyd Italiano passenger steamer "*Florida,*" with 830 survivors from the Messina earthquake aboard.

The damage sustained during the impact was causing the *Republic* to take on water and sink slowly. The decision was reached to transfer her passengers to the less damaged *Florida.** Jack Binns, the *Republic's* wireless operator, sent out a distress call received by the *Baltic*'s wireless operator, Henry J. Tattersall, and intercepted by Jack Irwin, the wireless operator at Marconi's land station Siasconsett, on Nantucket Island.

*(It is believed the S.S. "*Florida*" did not have a wireless transmitter or receiver.)

The *Baltic* then spent a fraught twelve hours searching for the drifting *Republic* and *Florida* and eventually, with the help of other vessels that had arrived in the vicinity, rescued the passengers and crew aboard *Florida.* It was the second, tension-filled lifeboat evacuation for the *Republic's* survivors. The next day, whilst under tow, *Republic* sank. The same day *Baltic* arrived back in New York with the survivors. Fate was yet to play a cruel hand for the *Baltic* when, on Sunday, April 14, 1912, the *Titanic,* on her maiden voyage, received customary wishes of success which also contained an ice warning from the *Baltic.* In circumstances, that were never satisfactorily explained, Captain Smith showed the cable to White Star Chairman J. Bruce Ismay, who then inexplicably placed it in his pocket, remaining in his possession until Captain Smith asked for it later. Only then was it posted in the chart room, casting serious doubt on Ismay's later claim that he was merely a passenger. The rest, as we know, is history.

Indeed, White Star vessels, on balance, enjoyed a great deal of exposure during the decades leading up to the loss of the *Titanic*, not all of it complimentary. In 1887, New Yorkers, readying themselves for the start of another week, would have been shocked when they read the early morning edition of the New York Times:
"Twelve Steerage Passengers Killed And Many Injured" ran part of the headline. The story went on;

> "A collision between the great steamers the Britannic and the Celtic, both of the White Star Line, occurred about 350 miles east of Sandy Hook in a thick fog Thursday afternoon about 5:25 o'clock. The Celtic was coming to New York, and the Britannic was on the second day of her journey to Liverpool. The movement of both vessels caused the Celtic to strike the Britannic no less than three times on the side, gouging a huge hole in her hull beneath the water line and inflicting other serious damage to both vessels. It is likely, that six steerage passengers on the Britannic were killed instantly by falling bars and plates of iron. Others are known to have been swept overboard and drowned. Careful investigation showed that certainly 12 lives, perhaps more, were lost and that 20 or more persons were injured."

Further on, the article, which filled more than half of the front page, said, "Purser Musgrove in his official statement covers the number lost with the word "several." The final death toll was never revealed. Even back then, the White Star Line only acknowledged first-class passengers who lost their lives.

(New York Times, May 23, 1887.)

According to the Report, the *Celtic* had about 870 cabin and steerage passengers on board. The *Britannic* carried some 450. The weather was foggy at the time, and the sea was calm. The fine line between luck and disaster that the White Star Line regularly straddled would be tested many times.

(Further reading: Britannic and Celtic Collide, 1887 (theshipslist.com)

The White Star Line, in common with other shipping lines, courted the Press by giving notice of ships' arrivals and departures, interviews with ship captains and releasing lists with prominent passengers names. This *quid pro quo* assuredly came with the understanding that when there was an adverse occurrence, the same newspapers clamoured for exclusivity and details of witnesses and company statements. One hand washes the other, so to speak. However, in this incident, the White Star Line was noticeably reticent. The New York Times dryly commented, "*The company's officers have not given accurate and full information. Purser Musgrove of the Britannic, the only officer of either vessel in the city last evening, made an indefinite statement.*" Navigation at sea, it appears, was not the only weak spot in the company's portfolio; they certainly never grasped the importance of good public relations when things 'went south.

Despite Sanderson's parochialism, the interval mentioned by the White Star Vice-President during his testimony before Lord Mersey began on the opposite side of the world with the loss of the 1,570 tons British steamer S.S. *Kaisari* from the Mogul Line, which sailed from Rangoon on November 23, for Reunion in the Indian Ocean and was wrecked during a hurricane. Twenty-five of the crew of 53 onboard the vessel, including the captain, were drowned. The period referred to came to a sad conclusion in July 1911 when the British cargo steamer S.S. *Fifeshire*, on route from Melbourne bound for London with 105 passengers and crew, was stranded with the loss of 24, of whom 10 were passengers.

(New York Times, January 18, 1901)
(Hocking, Charles, Dictionary of Disasters at Sea During the Age of Steam. Vol 1&II)

It appeared Davy Jones's locker* had no difficulty finding a watery sanctuary for distressed vessels wherever they were to be found.

(Referred to in "*Four Years Voyages of Capt. George Roberts*," Daniel Dafoe, 1726.)

Going further back in time, for the rejuvenated White Star Line, under the Chairmanship of Thomas Ismay, the early 1870s were to prove portentous in the success they enjoyed in the Trans-Atlantic passenger trade to North America. However, the company's relationship with the truculent conditions of the North Atlantic was to prove much harder to master. So many emigrants, noted the Irish Review in 1914, from many different ports of origin, were not only passengers in transit to the 'New World', but some were also to become reluctant travellers in transit to the next. The sobriquet 'coffin-ships' so often applied to emigrant vessels of the early Victorian period was to be replaced, in the closing stages of the same era, by another equally perilous epithet; 'Greyhounds of the Atlantic'.

(See: Our Seamen. An Appeal, by Samuel Plimsoll, M.P. Virtue & Co., London. 1873.)
(From "Coffin Ship " to "Atlantic Greyhound "*The Irish Review (Dublin)* Vol. 4, No. 37. March 1914)

Eighteenth-century diarist Samuel Johnson, who had an opinion on just about everything, and, it seems, had no good things to say about life at sea, is credited with saying;

> *"No man will be a sailor who has contrivance enough to get himself into jail; for being in a ship is being in a jail, with the chance of being drowned."*

(Life Of Johnson by James Boswell, 1791)

It was not only the open waters of the North Atlantic that proved difficult to negotiate for the passenger shipping lines, particularly the White Star Line. As vessels grew, not only in how fast they could travel but also in their sheer size and the space they occupied, then speed and displacement became problematical in congested coastal approaches to harbours and rivers in the shared confines with smaller, slower-moving craft. In those circumstances, there was only ever going to be one outcome. In his familiar bullish style Charles Lightoller, the Second Officer serving on the *Titanic* at the time of the collision, wrote many years later;

> "I had been with him (Smith) many years, off and on, in the mail boats, Majestic, mainly, and it was an education to see him con his own ship up through the intricate channels entering New York at full speed. One particularly bad corner, known as the South-West Spit, used to make us fairly flush with pride as he swung her round, judging his distances to a nicety; she is heeling over to the helm with only

a matter of feet to spare between each end of the ship and the banks."
(Titanic and Other Ships. Chapter Thirty. Loss Of The "Titanic " 1935)
Lightoller was probably also depicting the attitudes of many ship officers prevalent at the turn of the century. However, Lightoller's version bears an uncanny similarity to an article three decades earlier in the New York Times, on the occasion of the *Baltic*'s arrival in New York at the conclusion of her maiden voyage. A paragraph from the article read;

"Capt. Smith was delighted with his ship. "I tried to see how she would work coming around the tail of the Southwest Spit," he said, "and as the channel was clear, I sent her around at full speed. She behaved admirably. Pilot Johnson, who has brought up almost every one of the big vessels that came into this port, piloted us up."
(New York Times, July 9, 1904)

In a rare departure from his usual literary themes, Rudyard Kipling wrote, in the vernacular of the period, a novel, *Captain's Courageous*, published in 1897, about the son of a wealthy railroad tycoon, Harvey Cheyne Jr, who falls overboard from a passenger steamer and is rescued by a Portuguese dory fisherman, Manuel, off the Grand Banks where hardship and dangers are ever-present. After spending an edifying time at sea, the boy is reunited with his parents during which time the boy's father, speaks of the line of packet ships he has recently acquired, "*As straight as the winds let 'em, and I give a bonus for record passages. Tea don't improve by being at sea.*" (Authors Italics)

Even in a work of fiction, Kipling's penchant for authenticity reflects the ship owner's attitudes of the time. As if to punctuate the need for extra vigilance in congested waterways, on September 3, 1878, the pleasure ship *Princess Alice* (432grt) left Gravesend to travel up the River Thames for London, fully loaded with 900 people on board. Shortly after, she collided with the collier *Bywell Castle* (1,376 grt) and broke in two; the bow section of the *Princess Alice* sank immediately. The *Bywell Castle* dropped anchor but was too far away to be any practical help for rescue with lifeboats. The number of lives lost is generally assumed to be 640 persons. Those saved numbered a little over 200.

(Dictionary of Disasters at Sea During the Age of Steam: 1824-1962, Vol I&II. Charles Hocking, 1969)

This appalling disaster took place within a stone's throw of the banks of the river. The incident brought about changes and improvements in safety, but apparently 'stupid is as stupid does', and what seemed like a repeat of the circumstances of the tragedy occurred over a century later. In the early hours of the morning of August 20, 1989, the *Marchioness*, a vintage Thames pleasure cruiser with 131 people on board, was struck by the 262ft dredger *Bowbelle* (1,475 grt). The blow came firstly from behind, forcing her further into the path of the *Bowbelle*, causing her to roll and fill with water, which then passed over her, resulting in the deaths of 51 people.

Whether far out to sea or within coastal waterways, legislation or tribunals alone was not a deterrent to risk-taking or incompetence. With profits, perishable cargo, and fierce competition in the passenger-carrying trade at stake, fortune favoured the bold and the British Inquiry would expose the behaviour's that demonstrated such attitudes prevalent at the time.

"The most amazing wonder of the deep is its unfathomable cruelty.
(Joseph Conrad–*The Mirror of the Sea*. 1906. Chapter XXXVI.)

Most senior ships captains would come to realise their previous experience at sea would not prepare them for the peculiar demands of navigating large steam-powered vessels with handling characteristics that differed greatly from the smaller and slower ships they had served on as young officers. Some were never to learn to their cost.

The first of the quartet of 'Oceanic class' steamships, intended for Thomas Ismay's dreams of expansion, that came down the slipways of Harland and Wolfe's Belfast shipyard; *Oceanic, Atlantic, Baltic* and *Republic* all met with mixed success. The *Celtic* and *Adriatic*, were added later, launched in 1871.

Perhaps it was among these White Star vessels that Dr Caldwell, a Cunard ships surgeon, had in mind when he wrote his letter to the Nautical Magazine in 1876, warning of the potential consequences of the increase in speed of large steamships and the propensity for human error.

The truth of Dr Caldwell's remarks are almost self-evident and will be conceded;

"When one considers the increasing rate of speed as compared with the more leisurely progress of the days when steam was unknown." (Authors Italics)

Concluding;

"When the carrying trade is being absorbed by the swiftly moving steamer, and when collision between two of these monsters means such a frightful catastrophe, anything that tends to narrow this issue is worthy of careful consideration."
(Authors Italics)

Caldwell's own berth, R.M.S. *Russia*, herself capable of a respectable 14 knots, was soon outpaced by the new White Star fleet.

(Defective Vision, A Cause Of Disaster At Sea. The Nautical Magazine, 1877, Volume 46, pages 88-9.)

Dr Caldwell may inadvertently have been referring to another White Star vessel. In those early years, *Oceanic* enjoyed a relatively incident-free honeymoon period sailing on the Liverpool to New York route. In 1875, she was chartered to another shipping line for service in the Pacific between San Francisco, Yokohama, and Hong Kong. Not long after she commenced duties, in December 1876, she set a speed record for the Yokohama to San Francisco run and again in November 1889. The year before, on the return trip during one of those voyages from Hong Kong on August 22, 1888, the *Oceanic* (nearly 4,000 tons and 428 feet in length) collided with the steamship S.S. *City of Chester* (slightly over 1,100 tons and 202 feet in length) outward bound for Eureka, Cal. The collision occurred in daylight in thick, drifting fog, and although the waters were calm, there were strong currents on the approach to San Francisco harbour.*

Confusion followed when ships officers misinterpreted fog signals, and the whereabouts of both vessels to each other were uncertain in the narrow Channel. Response to the helm was slow in the strong ebb currents for both vessels, but the smaller *City of Chester* more so.

*(Work would not begin on the Golden Gate Bridge until 1933. The strait is known for fast-running tides, frequent storms, and fogs that made construction difficult.)

By the time both vessels took evasive action, it was too late; the *Oceanics'* bow plunged 10 feet into the much smaller *City of Chester's* forward port quarter, 30 feet aft of the bow. With the hull damaged below the waterline, she sank in under ten minutes, taking the lives of 13 men and women, one child and 3 crewmen. The British Consular investigation into the sinking concluded that the *Oceanic* was not blameworthy for the collision or the deaths of 16 adult passengers and crew. On the American side, there was the acceptance that both captains might have acted differently and could have avoided an accident. The U.S. Board of Pilot's Commissioners invited experienced witnesses to give their views. They concluded that the *Oceanic* should not have entered the confines of the Channel in poor visibility unless they were short of coal and should have anchored until conditions improved.

The relationship between the maritime bodies of both nations was strained and, in circumstances that were to bear a resemblance to certain events that unfolded following the sinking of the *Titanic,* remained so.

As mentioned previously, on June 8, 1871, the *Atlantic* left Liverpool on her maiden voyage to New York. Her career was to be brief. On March 20, 1873, on only her nineteenth trip, she left Liverpool for New York. After a series of fatal errors and bad decisions, in foul weather, she ran aground and sank off the coast of Nova Scotia, on April 1, 1873, with the tragic loss of over 500 people.

The *Adriatic* sailed on her maiden voyage on April 11, 1872, from Liverpool to New York. A month later, during a subsequent Atlantic crossing to New York, *Adriatic* maintained an average speed of slightly over 14.5 knots and won the Blue Riband from the Cunard's RMS *Scotia*, which she had held since 1866.

As the largest of the six White Star Line ships, *Adriatic* received the designation as the line's flagship until the larger, Britannic at 5,004 grt, was launched in February 1874, eventually taking the Blue Riband herself in 1876 with an average speed of just under 16 knots.

Although details are scarce, *Britannic* too was to have her share of incidents; on October 26, 1878, she ran down and sank the tugboat "*Willie*" on the Thames at Wapping whilst the tug was on a voyage from London to Dundee. Fortunately, there was no loss of life.

(List of shipwrecks in March 1869 - Wikipedia.
https://en.wikipedia.org/wiki/List_of_shipwrecks_in_March_1869)

On the night of March 31, 1881, she collided with and sank the schooner, "*Julia*," in the Mersey as she approached Liverpool;

> "There was a heavy current running, which had evidently taken the schooner out of her course. In an instant, she drifted against the starboard side of the steamer with a crash, and filled so rapidly that she went down before the other vessel could pass ahead of her."

Further on;

"A search was made for the persons belonging to the schooner. One boat returned without finding any traces of them, but when the second came alongside the officer in charge reported that he had hailed a brig which had picked up three men, the entire crew of the lost schooner, the name of which was not ascertained."
(New York Times, April 11, 1881.)

The White Star Line, at an early stage, understood the benefits of getting their version of the facts in first, ahead of everyone else.

There were no casualties, and the undamaged *Britannic* could continue her voyage. Later that year, on July 4, *Britannic* ran aground in fog off Kilmore, County Wexford, Ireland, en route to Liverpool and remained stuck for several days.

On April 5, 1885, another White Star vessel, *Germanic*, encountered a severe storm whilst crossing to New York with 850 passengers on board. On the second day of her voyage, she was struck by a large wave which broke over the ship causing substantial damage and 13 people were injured, with one sailor being washed overboard. The captain abandoned the journey, and the ship was turned around and returned to port in order for repairs to be carried out. Passengers were later conveyed from Queenstown to New York on the *City of Berlin* of the Inman Line and on the White Star's own *Adriatic*.
(Struck By Huge Waves. April 19, 1885, New York Times)
(www.norwayheritage.com)

In January 1890, the *Britannic* once again demonstrated how the presence of large steamers posed a serious threat to smaller vessels in coastal waters. On the inbound journey from New York in foggy conditions, the brigantine "*Czarowitz*" was run down by the *Britannic* in the Crosby Channel with the loss of her captain. Five of the remaining crew were rescued by the *Britannic's* lifeboats after the surviving crew clung to the ship's rigging.

(The Times, January 4, 1890.)
(Royal Cornwall Gazette - Thursday, January 9, 1890)

On 11 December 1895, in dense fog, the now elderly 5,008 grt White Star liner S.S. *Germanic* departed Liverpool for New York. Near the Crosby Channel at the entrance of the River Mersey she collided with the inbound 900grt *Cumbrae*, resulting in *Germanic's* bow penetrating about 12 feet into the side of the smaller ship. The *Cumbrae's* 28 passengers and crew had time to scramble aboard the embedded *Germanic* to safety. Shortly after, when the two vessels were parted, the *Cumbrae* rapidly sank. *Germanic's* bow was severely damaged, and she immediately returned to port, and was withdrawn from service for repairs. The *Germanic* had only recently returned to service following an extensive refit. Her propensity for calamity would become the object of public exhibition only a few years later.

(The Germanic In Collision. The Times, 12 December 1895.)

Mentioned previously and perhaps the most well-documented but least favourable to White Star's reputation, occurred on May 19, 1887, when the *Celtic* collided with *Britannic* in thick fog about 350 miles east of Sandy Hook.

During this early period of her sea-going career, the *Adriatic* became involved in several incidents. The first occurred on October 24, 1874, when she came into contact with the Cunard Line's S.S. *Parthia* as they were departing New

York, resulting in the *Adriatic* having to return to port to have repairs carried out, while the *Parthia* was able to continue on her voyage. The incident was reported with a hint of jingoistic disdain;
> "In steaming down the harbor, the White Star steamer Adriatic came up with the Parthia, and gradually drew ahead. When her stern was abreast of the bridge of the latter ship, she, for some reason, starboarded her helm. Seeing there was a great probability of the two ships fouling, the officers of the Parthia immediately put our helm hard-a-starboard, stopped and reversed the engines. Notwithstanding these efforts to keep clear, our starboard bow came into collision with the port quarter of the Adriatic, doing her some damage, but not hurting the Parthia more than a brush full of paint will remedy."

(New York Times October 27, 1874)

Presumably, the captain of the *Adriatic* (3,888grt.), proceeding as he did at pace to overtake the slower and slightly smaller vessel, *Parthia* (3,167grt.), had failed to take account of the suction effect created as the two ships passed in close proximity. This occurrence would not be the last time a White Star captain would fall foul of this phenomenon and come to grief.

The following year, on March 8, 1875, towards the end of a voyage from New York, the *Adriatic* collided with the schooner *Columbus* in the Crosby Channel near Liverpool. The schooner's captain, his wife, three crew members, and a pilot were rescued by the steamer *Enterprise*. However, during the desperate struggle, the captain's young child was lost. According to one newspaper article;

> "The vessel struck a three-masted schooner, dropped alongside, and gradually drifted away. The captain hailed and asked if they were much hurt but received no reply. When she was passing the stern the second mate hailed them, but no reply was received from either. The only light the captain saw was one burning in the cabin; there were no side lights when the vessel went clear. The Adriatic burnt rockets and blue lights, and two steamers came within hail. The captain told them the ship had been in collision with a vessel and asked them to go and see if assistance was wanted. Seeing they did as request he proceeded to the river. The Adriatic received no damage."

(The Yorkshire Herald – March 16, 1875.)

In his Report to the Receiver of Wrecks after docking at Liverpool, the *Adriatic*'s Captain Perry claimed that the *Columbus* was not showing any lights to the side. A sail was reported from the forecastle head; the helm was put hard to starboard, and the engines were stopped as soon as the vessel was seen. A formal Inquiry was held by the Admiralty Court on May 25 And 26 of the same year. It was reported;

> "His Lordship was of opinion that the master had given no reason to account for his not having lowered a boat, and so ascertained the extent of the damage, especially if, as the master said, he stayed by the schooner for about half an hour. His

Lordship said he acquitted the master of deliberate inhumanity but thought that the master must have lost his presence of mind and that if assistance had been rendered by those on board the steamship, the child's life might have been saved. As no reasonable excuse had been shown by the master for not remaining by the schooner, the collision must, under the provisions of the 33rd section of the Merchant Shipping Act Amendment Act, 1862, "*in the absence of proof to the contrary be deemed to have been caused by his wrongful act, neglect, or default.*" His Lordship then examined the evidence and came to the conclusion that there was no such proof to the contrary and that, therefore the Adriatic was alone to blame for the collision."
(The Times, May 27, 1875)

The difficulties associated with a large vessel in a narrow shipping channel were once again highlighted, when later that same year, in the early hours of December 31, 1875, in the proximity of St Georges Channel at the entrance to the Irish Sea, on the homeward leg of her voyage, the *Adriatic,* under the command of Captain Jennings, collided with and sank the Black Ball Line's vessel *Harvest Queen* (1383grt). A search of the area could find no trace of the *Harvest Queen's* crew of about 30.
(www.norwayheritage.com)

The *Harvest Queen's* owners tried to hold the White Star Line liable for losses; however, the *Adriatic* was found not to be responsible. The incident became another source of acrimony between the authorities in the U.S. and Great Britain. The New York Times reported;

"While the Harvest Queen was going up the Channel, she was run into by a steamer, about 3 o'clock on the morning of the 31st, with such violence as to crush in her port bow, causing her to sink almost immediately, and become, with her cargo, a total loss, and the officers and crew, and all on board, were drowned. Suit was begun in the Admiralty Court, in this district, by the owners of the Harvest Queen, alleging that the Adriatic was the vessel that ran into the Harvest Queen, and that the collision resulted from the negligence of those navigating the Adriatic, in not having a good lookout, in running at too great a rate of speed, in not keeping out of the way of the ship – as steamers are bound to do if possible when meeting sailing vessels – and not stopping and backing in time to avoid the collision; and the owners of the Harvest Queen sought to recover $225,000 damages. The answer was that the Harvest Queen was either sunk by a collision with some other vessel than the steamer or was wrecked. Judge Blatchford, before whom the case was tried, gave a decision yesterday, holding that the evidence established the fact the Adriatic was the vessel that collided with the Harvest Queen, but he holds further that the Harvest Queen changed her course and lights in such a manner that the Adriatic was entirely deceived as to her intentions, and could not be held

responsible for the collision. He concludes that the Adriatic "could act only in view of what she saw, and what she had a right reasonably to infer form what she saw. Her movements were taken with a reasonable certainty that they would give safety to both vessels. She exercised that diligence directly, throughout to the end, in all the emergencies which the vacillating movements of the ship threw upon her. The libel is dismissed with costs."
(The Harvest Queen Disaster. New York Times April 29, 1877)

On July 19, 1878, *Adriatic* was said to have collided with the barque *Hengist,* 18 miles off Holyhead in dense fog;

"It was reported that the Adriatic had been in collision with another vessel which was in tow of a Liverpool tug, and had carried away her side lights, but the agents at Queenstown made no allusion to this circumstance, and our correspondent had no confirmation of the report. "
(Glasgow Herald - Monday, July 22, 1878)

Incredibly, later that same day, the *Adriatic* collided with and sank another vessel, the brig, *G. A. Pyke*, (171grt), off the coast of South Wales, with the loss of five of her crew; one member of the *G.A. Pyke's* crew survived and was picked up by a lifeboat from the *Adriatic.* (3887grt) The blame was fixed on *Adriatic* for excessive speed. However, the Glasgow Herald newspaper carried the story and part of the article stated;

"From the statement of her agents at Queenstown, it appears that the Adriatic, when coming down Channel experienced a dense fog on Friday morning. It was in consequence deemed prudent to stop the vessel about ten o'clock when the fog was densest. The brigantine, which was bound from Gravesend to Dublin with cement, came into collision with the steamer, and sank immediately after."

(Glasgow Herald - Monday, July 22, 1878)

It seems from this account that the White Star Line was claiming that the *Adriatic* was stationary at the time of the collision, and the *G.A. Pyke* ran into her and sank! However, the official Inquiry into the collision stated;

"That the collision was due to the great speed at which the steamer "Adriatic" was being navigated during the dense fog that prevailed at the time, and which made it impossible for her to avoid the brigantine "G.A. Pyke" after she was seen."

In the Report of Court, it was further stated;

"The Court of opinion that John William Jennings, the master of the "Adriatic," was to blame for not having taken measures to ascertain the speed of the vessel; for having supposed her to be going at from 5 to 6 knots an hour, when in fact she was going from 9 to 10 knots; and for having allowed a speed of only 5 knots an hour to be inserted in the log-book as that of the "Adriatic" although he well knew, from having ascertained her positioned at noon of that day and the distance run, that her speed must have been nearly double that recorded.

For these wrongful acts and defaults, the Court considers that the said John William Jennings is greatly to blame, but looking to the careful attention which he paid to the navigation of the vessel in other respects and to the promptness with which the orders were given after the "G.A. Pyke" was made out, and with which the boats were lowered after the collision, it returns him his certificate, at the same time warning him to be more careful in future.

The Court is further of the opinion that William Sowden, the third officer, and John Pascoe, the fourth officer of the "Adriatic" were guilty of carelessness in superintending the heaving of the log, but it returns them their certificates with a warning to be more careful in future."

A token slap on the wrist for the wrongful death of 5 sailors and an attempt to falsify the logbook of the ship's actual speed in dense fog, particularly as this was not the first time Captain Jennings stood accused of wrongdoing. Those who felt they had cause to question the integrity of inquiries into shipping losses would have much to consider in light of these findings.

> *"They that go down to the sea in ships, and occupy their business in great waters;*
> *These men see the works of the Lord, and his wonders in the deep."*

(Psalm 107, verses 23,24)

Twenty years before Sir Walter Howell would present dubious figures on shipping losses before Lord Mersey's Inquiry, Glasgow M.P. Dr Charles Cameron asked the then

President of the Board of Trade, Sir Michael Hicks Beach in Parliament;

> "Whether, when speaking at the dinner of the Chamber of Shipping of the United Kingdom, he stated that the loss of life at sea had been reduced to 1 in 256, he was speaking of the total loss of life at sea from all causes, or whether he was speaking of the loss of life under two headings alone of several under which the loss of life at sea is classified; and what were the headings under which loss of life at sea are classified which were not included by him in the figures he gave?"

Hicks Beach replied;

> "When speaking on the occasion to which the hon. Member refers, I was not stating the "total loss of life at sea from all causes," but, as I clearly explained, only the loss of life among seamen arising from wrecks and casualties at sea to merchant ships registered in the United Kingdom—namely, lives lost in direct consequence of accidents causing total loss or damage to the ships. The corresponding figures for 1881 are 1 in 79. The loss of life which is not included in the foregoing figures was that which occurred from drowning and other accidents, although the ships were in no way damaged or in danger."

(Loss Of Life At Sea. HC Deb 17 March 1892 vol 2 c1059)

Although the absence of context in the President's remarks makes it difficult to substantiate the accuracy of his claims it appears there was some selective adjustments made to the losses figures to make them appear less significant. Interestingly, a certain Walter Howell, whose name would be associated with later accusations of deception, was then Private Secretary to Hicks-Beech and may have had a hand in preparing his speech.

An article in the "The Life-Boat" quarterly journal for the period states;

"On reference to the latest statistics, we find that during the year 1881-82 there were no less than 3,660 shipping disasters immediately around and on the coasts of the United Kingdom, exceeding the total of the previous year by 85, and resulting in the lamentable loss of 1,097 lives the corresponding number for the year 1880-81 being 984. This total of 3,660 wrecks includes all sorts and classes of maritime accidents, viz., wrecks involving total loss, partial loss, collisions, &c., and it is a matter for satisfaction to know that the cases of total loss declined from 705 to 605, and those resulting in loss of life, from 238 to 235, so that the remaining 3,054 casualties may be looked upon as less serious."

Further on the article states;

"The 8,660 shipping disasters which occurred off the coasts of the United Kingdom during the year 1881-2, comprised 4,367 vessels. Unfortunately, the number of ships is larger than the total of the previous year by 70; it exceeds the casualties reported, because in cases of collision two or more ships are necessarily involved in one casualty. Thus

686 were collisions, and 2,974 were wrecks and casualties other than collisions. 526 of these latter disasters were wrecks, &c., resulting in total loss; 719 were casualties resulting in serious damage, and 1,729 were minor accidents."

In closing the article said;

"The Wreck Abstract again shows a very considerable increase in the number of lives lost during the year. Last year we recorded 984, now we have to report, 1,097. Of these, 319 were lost in vessels that foundered, 77 through vessels in collision, 302 in ships stranded or cast ashore, and 300 in missing vessels. The remaining 99 lives were lost from various causes, such as through being washed overboard in heavy seas, explosions, &c. Of the 235 ships from which the 1,097 lives were lost, 215 were British, involving the loss of 1,021 lives, and 20 were foreign, causing the loss of 76 lives."

(The Wreck Register and Chart For 1881-82. The Journal of the National Life-Boat Institution November I, 1883. Vol. XII. No. 130. p209)

The figures mentioned in the above article are at variance with those quoted by Hicks-Beach in his reply to Dr Cameron. It would not be the last time statistics quoted by a senior representative of the Board of Trade for shipping casualties and loss of life would be open to question. As a campaigning politician, among other things, for stricter liquor licensing laws in Scotland, one can assume Dr Cameron's question was intended as a sober reflection on the loss of life at sea.

Nonetheless, Sir Robert Finlay had scored an important point in his depiction of the White Star Lines record of travel across the North Atlantic and succeeded in impressing on the mind of Lord Mersey the perceived low incidence of passenger fatalities.

Sail Gives Way to Steam

Joseph Turner's painting, *The Fighting Temeraire* completed in 1838 and revealed to the public the following year, showed one of the last surviving ships that took part in the Battle of Trafalgar in 1805. The former 98-gun ship of the line, her masts removed, is depicted being towed ignominiously along the Thames to the breaker's yard by a steam-driven tugboat, smoke billowing forth, threatening to blacken the ochre hues. The oils of the setting sun encapsulated the once-proud vessel being led to its inevitable end, symbolically flying a white flag, not of surrender but resignation. The age of steam, it seemed, was in ascendance, yet it would take another three decades before the first of Thomas Ismay's vessels would take to the sea.

As if to emphasise the changing times, Isambard Kingdom Brunel launched the S.S. *Great Britain* a mere five years after Turner painted the *Temeraire*. Although *Great Britain* had a steam engine, it also had masts and sails. In time those would be gone as well. Symbolically, it was the beginning of a new era. Steam-driven machinery was used in factories, mines, railways and now ships. *Great Britain* marked a milestone in the development of steam as a means of propulsion. Unlike Coleridge's *Ancient Mariner*, ships at sea would no longer be held captive to the vagaries of the weather.

Who Breaks A Butterfly Upon A Wheel?

"Oh, what a tangled web we weave.
When first we practice to deceive."

(Marmion: A Tale of Flodden Field. Sir Walter Scott. 1808.)

Chief of the Marine Department, Walter J. Howell, a 40-year veteran of the Board of Trade, was the first senior Board of Trade official to appear before Lord Mersey, followed five days later by Sir Norman Hill, Chairman of the Merchant Shipping Advisory Committee. Both were asked about shipping losses in broadly the same period. As Chief of the Marine Department of the Board of Trade, Walter "Jack" Howell had token seniority over Sir Norman Hill, however, both presumably, had access to the same nautical data on shipping casualties, yet both produced quite different interpretations. The questioning of Sir Walter Howell by the Attorney-General suggested careful choreography, the purpose of which appears to elicit responses that concentrated solely on Trans-Atlantic voyages with UK-owned passenger vessels.

Although the Inquiry was tasked with investigating the loss of a large passenger liner in the north-Atlantic, the general rules of construction and navigation regulating these vessels applied to all passenger-carrying merchant vessels and if, for instance, it was discovered that there was a flaw in design or manufacture then there would, presumably, following the Inquiry, be changes made to these regulations which by default, might ultimately affect all merchant vessels. The cost, of course, of any such recommendations being borne by the ship owners. Following the Inquiry, an excellent example was the voluntary on the part of the White Star Line, extensive structural alterations to the *Titanic*'s sister ship, the *Olympic*.

As with Harold Sanderson's numbers, which were seen to be biased solely towards the White Star Line, the sources being quoted by both these influential Board of Trade civil servants were not, as far as can be discerned, formally entered into the minutes of evidence, except through testimony alone and there were striking differences between both witnesses sets of numbers.

It appears that most of those present in the Scottish Drill Hall during the Inquiry from the assembled legal counsel and advisors, members of the Press and public accepted those figures without question, together with *Titanic* historians ever since.

If we are to examine the claims made by these witnesses with a scrupulous eye and compare them with Lloyd's Shipping Register in which case, the narrative becomes weighted by figures which conflict with evidence given before Lord Mersey and requires further scrutiny.

Historically, the responsibility for maintaining a Wreck Register was taken over by the Marine Department of the Board of Trade by the Merchant Shipping Act of 1854. From 1856, the Board of Trade published abstracts of the wrecks and casualties (Casualty Returns), of which it was notified. While the content varied over time, the abstracts consistently included information such as the dates and circumstances of losses.

(www.rmg.co.uk/researchers/library/research-guides/the-merchant-navy/wrecks-losses-and-casualties.)
(Lloyd's Register Casualty Returns: Lloyd's Register Foundation, Heritage & Education Centre: Internet Archive)
The U.K. National Archives contains a file, which is a collection; "of papers prepared in connection with the loss of the S.S. *Titanic*." Evidently, this document is a set of briefing notes, presumably for legal counsel representing the Board of Trade during the Inquiry.
(MT 9/920F No 365. M25522 pages103-374)
Within this file (pages 262-331) is Departmental Paper No 255; which is headed: -
"Statistics compiled in connection with the S.S. "Titanic" Inquiry showing loss of life in the British Trans-Atlantic passenger trade."
The information contained within these documents broadly matches that which was stated by Sir Walter Howell in his testimony before Lord Mersey. From that, it is reasonable to conclude that both are one and the same. In considering the importance of their content to the Inquiry, there is no persuasive reason why these documents, arguably, of at least equal public interest and historical significance, should have been excluded from Lord Mersey's Final Report. Especially, when others, for example, Section 6 of the Report* went to inordinate lengths to justify the Board of Trade's apparent stasis since 1894 when the Merchant Shipping Act became law and in the intervening years the size of ships were already exceeding "10,000 tons and upwards" such as the Lucania at 12,952grt while the number of lifeboats under davits remained rooted at 16. Otherwise, why leave them out?

Department Paper No 246 "Memorandum on the Statutory Requirements as to Life-Saving Appliances " (pages 265-302) contains documents which were reproduced in Section 6 of the Final Report which concerned the Board of Trade's Administration; where letters and tables from the same briefing notes portfolio were reproduced in the Report by way of supporting evidence.

Howell was to be questioned by the Attorney-General, who apparently had little interest in getting to the substance behind these numbers, only, it seemed, to place them on record.

The Attorney-General began his questioning;

"I want you to direct your attention to some figures which have been compiled with reference to the number of passengers who lost their lives over a period of years on voyages from the United Kingdom to America. The point of it is that the Court may have before it what did happen during the 20 years that preceded this accident, and it has a material bearing of course upon the recommendations that ought to have been made and that were made."

He continued;

"Will you take first of all the 10 years from 1892 to 1901? The total number of passengers carried inward and outward between the United Kingdom and the United States and British North America on all ships - that is, both British and foreign ships, was over 3 1/4 millions? - That is so."

The questioning went on;

"And of those 3 1/4 million passengers was the great proportion carried in ships belonging to the United Kingdom? - By far the greater proportion."
Will you give me the number of passengers who during that period of ten years lost their lives by casualties to vessels belonging to the United Kingdom? - From the years 1892 to 1901, the number of passengers lost by casualties to vessels at sea was - Belonging to the United Kingdom? - Belonging to the United Kingdom was of passengers - west-bound 66, east-bound 7.
Seventy-three in all? - Seventy-three in all."
Plainly the Attorney-General was leading the witness by the hand through the evidence.
He continued;
"Have you also considered the figures for the ten years 1902 to 1911? - Yes.
Was the number of passengers carried under the same conditions by both British and foreign ships over six millions? - Over six millions.
And of those six millions was the greater proportion carried by vessels belonging to the United Kingdom? - Certainly; far the greater proportion."
The Attorney-General continued;
"Now, will you give me the number of passengers who lost their lives by casualties at sea in vessels belonging to the United Kingdom? - West-bound 8, east-bound 1.
Nine in all during that ten years? - Nine in all."

> I suppose it is not possible for you to give the figures with regard to the total which you have given because that includes both the British and foreign ships? - Yes. I want to be very careful to point that out.
> You only have the figures available for vessels belonging to the United Kingdom? - Quite so."

(Brit Inq 22142-153)

Why did the Attorney-General request the total number of passengers carried "*on all ships - that is, both British and foreign ships,*" and then only include "*the number of passengers who lost their lives by casualties at sea in vessels belonging to the United Kingdom?*"

Sir Rufus Isaacs then queries if Sir Walter Howell only has numbers of casualties on British vessels and when told in the affirmative, he moves on without comment. Was this a serious omission on his part or an acceptance of the figures as presented? As we shall see there were a great many lives lost from vessels out with the United Kingdom, although many were built in British yards and destined for ports in North America.

When it is considered that the loss of the vessel being investigated by this Inquiry, i.e., the *Titanic*, which did not "*belong to the United Kingdom*" the Attorney-General appears to have his judicial 'wires crossed' so to speak.

The Attorney-General concludes by confirming the source of his information;

> "I have a Table, My Lord, which I have summarised, giving you what I think are the material figures, but I have a Table here for every year,

showing them exactly. It did not seem to me that that was necessary. The total is what is required."
There is no reference in the Inquiry transcripts as to any of the "Tables" being handed in for inclusion in the Final Report.

The Attorney-General continued, demonstrating a certain impatience;

"Yes. I might exhaust the figures as we are upon them. I do not want to go back to them. I am only going to give the summary. Will you just tell me whether this is right: For the 10 years ending June 30, 1881, there were 822 lives, crew, and passengers, lost? I am going back, as your Lordship sees, to an earlier period, and I am including crew. The figures I gave just now were only dealing with passengers. For the next 10 years ending June 30, 1891, were there 247 lives, crew, and passengers, lost? - From July 1, 1881, to June 30, 1891, three vessels and 247 lives."

Continuing the Attorney-General stated;

"That includes crew and passengers? - That includes crew and passengers. I thought it was not quite right to confine my observations with regard to statistics simply to passengers, and I compiled these figures to give them both with regard to crew and passengers.

Quite right. And then to June 30, 1901, that is carrying the period forward for another 10 years - 183 lives, crew, and passengers, were lost? - Yes.

That would compare with the figure of 73 which you gave us first, would it not? The 183 would include the 73? - It would include the 73, yes.
It is the same period? - It is the same period.
So that you have got seventy-three passengers and that would mean 110 crew? - Quite so.
Then for the next period to June 30, 1911, there were fifty-seven? - Fifty-seven lives lost.
Of which as we know there were nine passengers? - Yes. There is one remark I ought to make here. This only includes casualties through which over fifty lives were lost.
I was going to ask you that. Does that apply to both sets of figures which you have given us? You have given us first of all the passengers, and then you have given us the crew and passengers?
In the first there is no reservation, I think, with regard to the fifty lives lost.
That stands altogether apart from the calculation you have made? - Yes.
That is both the seventy-three and the nine? - Quite.
But in this later Table of the forty years which you have given, that only deals with casualties in which over fifty lives were lost. Is that right? - That is quite right.
I think we understand how that stands, and I do not think we need burden the Court with further figures upon that."
(Brit Inq 22156-168)

There was no explanation why only those incidents where more than 50 lives were lost were included, leaving one to conclude that there were possibly many more unaccounted-for victims involved in incidents. Either way, the Attorney-General was obviously in hurry to get past this part of the testimony.

"*I do not think we need burden the Court with further figures upon that.*" He had said dismissively. Another explanation for the repetition of the losses before Lord Mersey would become apparent.

The Attorney-General went on;

> "Then "Passenger steamers" is defined in the statute under the merchant Shipping Act, 1894, and to some extent also by the act of 1906, but substantially it includes every steamship, British or foreign, carrying passengers from, to, or between places in the United Kingdom? - Quite so. That is the substance of it - I am not using the exact words."

(Brit Inq 22156-170)

This explanation by the Attorney-General, "*not using the exact words,*" seems strange given that not all vessels, British or foreign, carrying passengers would stop at a port in the United Kingdom en route to destinations across the North Atlantic but still be classed as "passenger steamers" under the provisions of the relevant Acts.

The question becomes more complicated when emigrant vessels are in a separate class again. A passenger might be defined as someone who intends to make a return trip and is undertaking the voyage for business or pleasure. An emigrant however is self-explanatory. The point at which an emigrant is not considered a "passenger," even on a designated emigrant vessel becomes complicated.

A case in point might be the Cunard lines S.S. *Carpathia*, which began a voyage that would take her to New York on March 4, 1912, from Trieste, on the Adriatic Sea, and on to four other Mediterranean ports before departing Gibraltar, leaving the 'Pillars of Hercules' in her wake for the dash across the Atlantic and not stopping at any ports in the U.K. In which case, *Carpathia* was a British vessel, and according to Captain Rostron's evidence before the U.S. Senate Inquiry, carrying approximately; 150 first; 50 second; and about 560 or 575 third class passengers to New York, but not from a U.K. port, therefore, had she foundered due to some mishap at sea, she would not, according to the first part of the Attorney-General's question, have been included in these tables; however, his later persistent emphasis on only vessels "*belonging to the United Kingdom,*" she would have.

The *Carpathia's* return trip was, on that fateful occasion, delayed due to a certain vessel, the *Titanic's* frantic calls for assistance, the rescue of the survivors from the ill-fated ship and her captain's subsequent appearance before the U.S. Senate inquiry, now feted as a hero.

Notably absent from either Sir Walter Howell's or the Attorney-General's reckoning was the Anchor Lines S.S. *Utopia*; when she was en route from Trieste to New York in March 1891, she foundered in the bay of Gibraltar following a collision with H.M.S. *Anson,* and 562 out of a total complement of 860 lost their lives. Two rescuers,

James Cotton and George Hales, from the nearby naval vessel H.M.S. *Immortalité*, lost their lives during rescue attempts. Even today, the accounts of witnesses, survivors and rescuers make harrowing reading. Another aspect of the sinking was apportioning accountability for the loss.

"Capt. McKeague of the "Utopia," who was arrested yesterday charged with "wrongful acts, improper conduct, negligence, and mismanagement, " and who was released on bail the same day, was formally charged this morning before a magistrate. In addition to the charges against him already mentioned, he is accused of feloniously slaying certain persons unknown. He was admitted to bail in the amount of £480."

(New York Times, March 21, 1891)

On March 23, 1891, a Marine Court convened in Gibraltar.

"The duty of the Court will be to decide whether your certificate, conferred under the provisions of the Marchant Shipping Acts, 1854 to 1880, shall be suspended or cancelled."

The next day the Court's decision reads as follows;

"The Court are unanimously of opinion that the master of the steamship "Utopia," John McKeague, committed a grave error of judgment, by which his ship was sunk, and loss of life occurred."

Adding further on;

"The Court having further heard the evidence of the two Italian passengers, and the address of counsel for the defence, and also of Her Majesty's Attorney-General, who appeared for the Government, are unanimously of opinion (sic) that the decision already recorded sufficiently marks the finding of the Court, and that it is not deemed by the Court necessary to deal in any way with the master's certificate."

(Wreck Report (No. 4276.) "Utopia " (S.S.) And H.M.S. "Anson.")

One cannot help but wonder, had Captain Smith survived the foundering of the *Titanic*, whether an altogether different reception would have met the *Carpathia* on her arrival in New York and the prospect of him being led away under arrest, like Capt. McKeague of the Utopia, in front of an angry crowd.

As unfortunate as his death was, the British Inquiry into the sinking of the *Titanic* was spared the dilemma of how to deal with Captain Smith. Considering the long list of charges levelled against Captain McKeague, for his part in the loss of the *Utopia*, the Court found a "*grave error of judgement*" was all he was answerable for. Any sanctions, such as suspension of his certificate, were not deemed "*necessary*," and he went on his way, undoubtedly chastened by the whole experience. As it was in 1912, Lord Mersey could then paper over the cracks in Smith's flawed judgement as "*a mistake, a very grave mistake.*" Although the death toll in his case was considerably higher, begging the question exactly how many lives were needed to be lost to constitute negligent navigation?

In comparison to the judicial hounding of Captain Lord of the *Californian*, where the powers that be sought to sacrifice his career and reputation on the altar of public opinion in their quest to apportion blame, the findings of both these other Courts are remarkable in their leniency.

With the *Utopia*, one single loss, greater than any of the 10 cases cited by Sir Walter Howell for the period July 1, 1871, to June 30, 1901. Had this one casualty alone been included somewhere in these tables, the loss of life would have reflected negatively on the Board of Trade and their claims of Trans-Atlantic passage "*with remarkable immunity from loss of life*" being called into question.

This alleged "*safety record*," often quoted by counsel for the White Star Line, among others, of vessels crossing the Atlantic, could be construed as being inaccurate or, worse, deliberately false. The Attorney-General was wearing his Board of Trade hat when he asked the questions. His usual forensic examination of witness testimony during this segment was noticeably absent in his one-sided discourse with the witness.

It could be interpreted that Sir Rufus Isaacs needed the figures on the court records but not in the form of the actual tables themselves, only the sanitised figures, without context. However, as we shall discover, the *Utopia* loss was not the only calamity to have occurred and elude the Court's attention. What was so unusual about the ill-fated *Utopia* that kept it from the scrutiny of the British Inquiry? She was a British-registered passenger vessel with watertight bulkheads, wireless communications, 'filled to the gunnels' with emigrants and typically with insufficient lifeboats and lookouts. Except, she set out from Trieste, not Liverpool, Southampton, or any other U.K. port.

The figures alluded to by Sir Walter Howell suggest his responses to the Attorney-General's question were based on Page 264, showing Table 2 of the Board of Trade notes.

Table showing, for each of the years 1892 to 1911 inclusive, the number of passengers embarked in the United Kingdom for ports in the United States or British North America, and the number of passengers landed in the United Kingdom from the United States or British North America, with the number of passengers whose lives were lost owing to casualties to the vessels conveying them on such voyages:

The breakdown of the 66 lives mentioned who died on the west-bound route during the period 1892-1901 appears to be gleaned from pages 304-31 of the briefing notes which accounts for the losses among the following casualties:

(MT 9/920F No 365. M25522 pages103-374)
(Statistics as to loss of life (passengers and crew) in the Transatlantic passenger trade from 1872 to June 1911—compiled from Wreck Abstracts.)

In 1892, two lives were lost from the schooner *Clara*. The records for 1893 show eight lives lost, some of which was likely from the *Pomeranian*, whose deck was swept by a large wave in the North Atlantic, which took the lives of 7 crew members and five passengers. In 1898, the highest annual count, where 45 lives were lost, comprised of 23 crew and one passenger from the *Almida* and three crewmen who were swept overboard in 3 separate incidents and a fourth crewman on another vessel who was dragged overboard by heavy equipment during a storm at sea and lost.

One crewman was lost from the tanker *Vindobala* when she was abandoned before capsizing in heavy seas, mid-Atlantic and the remaining crew were rescued by the *Paris*. Included in the Board of Trade records for 1898, but not counted in Howell's totals, with five lives lost, was the schooner *Lady Bertha*, which went down, close to her destination, in gale force winds with all hands in Clear's Cove, Newfoundland on a journey from Alicante to St John's, Newfoundland. Sir Walter Howell did not mention that the lives of 111 officers and crew were lost in those same shipping casualties. Similarly, as in other years, officers and crew members were not always included in these calculations. Of those seven passengers whom Sir Walter Howell claimed had lost their lives on the eastbound route in the decade 1892-1901: -

Two of which appear to be from the *Peter Stuart*, which got stranded on rocks in heavy seas near Yarmouth NS, on a voyage from St John's N.B. to Liverpool in 1892 with the loss of two passengers and 12 crew, 13 were saved by the ship's own lifeboats. The risks of transporting flammable goods were driven home when, on October 17, 1898, towards the end of a voyage from New York to London, an explosion occurred aboard the British barque *Blengfell*, off Margate, Kent, which cost nine lives; that of the captain, his wife and child, all the officers, two apprentices, a crewman and the Dover pilot.

(old-merseytimes.co.uk)

There is no other record in the briefing notes of the remaining passengers said to have been lost on eastbound voyages. There are, however, other references to crew members lost on the eastbound route in the Board of Trade notes, some of whom include:

One crewman from the *Bath City* inbound from New York in 1900 was lost when she ran aground onto the Needle Rocks in the Bristol Channel. The 26 remaining crewmembers were saved by the ship's boats. In 1896, the steamer *Memphis* crossing from Montreal for Avonmouth was lost in Dunlough Bay, Co. Cork, from a crew of 33 and 14 cattlemen; nine of the crew were lost, and two cattlemen. The tables explain that 30 were saved by the ship's own boats; three by being taken from the rigging by boat from shore; two by being lowered onto a rock and being rescued by fishermen; the ship's master by getting ashore on a cattle fitting door!

On November 29, 1898, the British cargo vessel S.S. *Londonian*, from Boston to London with a cargo of grain and 150 head of cattle, ran into a gale, and began to take on water and was abandoned in the mid-Atlantic. Despite heroic efforts by the crew of the S.S. *Vedamore* to assist, she eventually sank with the loss of 17 of her crew of 70.
(Sea-Toll of our Time. R.L. Hadfield. The Nautilus Library. 1935)

Sixty miles off Cape Race, heading for Portmadoc, the barque *Hope* was lost in hurricane-force winds, and only three of the crew of nine survived. An explosion on board the S.V. *Norcross* cost the lives of nine near Honfleur, in the River Seine on November 4, 1892, while on a voyage from Philadelphia to Rouen with petroleum & naphtha and foundered. In total, a further 44 lives were unaccounted for in the figures quoted.

The figure of eight passengers lost on the west-bound route in the years 1902-1911 is inaccurate from the point of view of the Board of Trades' notes, which from 1909 records the

Republic collision as three passengers lost, not two, as was stated previously by Harold Sanderson. However, the total for the period 1902 to 1911 in the chart on page 264 of the notes shows that the lives of eight passengers were lost on the trip west and one from the *Nicaraguan* in 1907 on the eastbound return voyage to Dublin. The other vessels where lives were lost were the *Huronian* (1) and *Campania*. (5)

Unlike the numbers mentioned initially of those lost on the *Titanic*, where the discrepancies were understandable in the confusion that followed, there were also errors and omissions from the Board of Trade tables, which are also understandable as there is a vast amount of information available, and record-keeping was probably patchy at best. However, the mistake in the number of those who were killed, even if it happened days after the event, as a result of the Republic collision is favourable to prolonging the fiction portrayed by counsel for the White Star Line and is crucial to the accuracy of the Inquiry records is improper. The error in this case, is mentioned, almost like a badge of credit, by Sir Robert Finlay before the Court.

Over many years, there were several attempts to bring the accounts of losses at sea to a wider audience. In 1899 one campaigner for improved safety at sea, Mr Havelock-Wilson; M.P. for Holmfirth raised the matter in the House of Commons;

"I beg to ask the President of the Board of Trade whether he is aware that the following British registered steamships have foundered or are missing since June 1898:

Eira, Tina, Harbinger, Arno, Earnock, Almida, Recepta, Dora Foster, Caradoc, Arona, Laughton, Wooler, Boadicea, Picton, Oberon, City of Wakefield, Croft, Port Melbourne; also, that the following British registered sailing vessels foundered or are missing since June 1898: *Celtic Bard, Rose, Montague, Marlborough, Village Belle, Iddesleigh, Aldboro, Sunbeam, Dora, Andelina, Sefton, Hawkesdale, Dechmont, Laurel Bank, David Morgan, Atlanta*; and,

Whether he can state the number of persons carried on these vessels as crew or passengers, and the number who lost their lives on such vessels; and whether any inquiries have been held to ascertain the cause of the loss of these vessels, and in how many of these cases have no inquiries been held."

Mr Ritchie; (President of the Board of Trade)

"The list of steamships foundered or missing, as given in the question, is correct, except with regard to the Harbinger, which is reported to have arrived on the 3rd instant, the Arno, which was lost by stranding, and the Caradoc and Boadicea which were sailing vessels—not steamers. The list of sailing ships foundered or missing is correct, except with regard to the Dechmont, which is reported to be now on her voyage from Caleta Buena to London, the Sefton and the Hawkesdale which were lost by stranding, and the Marlborough which was lost in April 1898 (not since June 1898).

The number of persons carried on the vessels who were lost was 605 (including one passenger, the wife of a master), and the number of persons lost was 545, including the passenger. In six cases (Arno, Earnock, Wooler, Montagu, Hawkesdale, and Atalanta), formal inquiries have been held. In one case (Recepta), Inquiry was ordered but had to be abandoned for want of evidence. In three cases (Caradoc, Celtic Bard, and Laurelbank), inquiries have been ordered and are pending. In the remaining cases mentioned in the question, all available information was obtained by the Board of Trade; but the Department were of the opinion, after consideration of such information, that normal inquiries would be without useful result."

Undeterred Mr Havelock Wilson said;

"May I ask the right hon. Gentleman why no inquiry was held with regard to the loss of the eight steamers which foundered in January and February last in the Atlantic Ocean?"

(Loss Of Vessels At Sea. HC Deb August 07, 1899, vol 76 cc31-3)

One comment in the President's response is startling in that he states;

"*All available information was obtained by the Board of Trade; but the Department were of the opinion, after consideration of such information, that normal inquiries would be without useful result.*" (Authors Italics)

A further examination of the information given in his reply shows that in 20 cases no formal inquiry was undertaken. The relevant sections of the Act* stipulates that when a shipping casualty occurs, whether this involves loss of life or not, and evidence or witnesses can be found "in the

United Kingdom" then a preliminary inquiry may be conducted by local coastguard or customs officials, or: "In any case by any person appointed for the purpose by the Board of Trade." The next section explains further;
> "A person authorised as aforesaid to make a preliminary inquiry shall in any case where it appears to him requisite or expedient (whether upon a preliminary inquiry or without holding such an inquiry) that a formal investigation should be held, and in any case where the Board of Trade so directs, apply to a court of summary jurisdiction to hold a formal investigation, and that court shall thereupon hold the formal investigation."

*(Merchant Shipping Act, 1894. Part VI. Special Shipping Inquiries And Courts. Inquiries and Investigations as to Shipping Casualties. 464-479)

Revealingly, the criteria for recommending a formal investigation are not listed. Neither are the qualifications or credentials of such persons "*appointed for the purpose by the Board of Trade.*" This leaves the spirit, if not the letter, of the Act open to interpretation as to who makes the call on which shipping casualties should be investigated. Ships reported as missing with no survivors, therefore no witnesses, are most often those most likely to be "*without useful result.*" In those 36 incidents mentioned in the Commons question, the President of the Board of Trade states that 545 lives were lost in a matter of months. Not even when there is loss of life do relatives always get to find out the circumstances. Many death certificates would simply record, 'Missing at sea, presumed drowned.'

As we shall see, loss of life among seafarers plying their trade at sea was considered an occupational hazard and not an issue of great concern. Even though the matter was raised in Parliament, it was really only newsworthy when the lives of passengers were lost en masse and even then, for the shipping lines, largely only those in first class. This sent out a message to ship owners that if you overload your vessels or send your ships to sea in an unseaworthy condition and they sink, it is likely the circumstances will not be investigated.

Even those cases which result in an Inquiry often 'wither on the vine'. The case of the Berlin in 1907 supports that belief.

The 1,775 grt S.S. *Berlin* was owned by the Great Eastern Railway and intended for use on their ferry service between Harwich and the Hook of Holland, which the company had begun in 1893. In the early hours of the 21 February 1907 during a severe storm the vessel became impaled on the toe of the North Pier breakwater. Pounded by heavy seas the vessel eventually broke in two. Despite being so close to port nothing could be done to affect a rescue of those aboard until 1.30 pm the following day when the winds had moderated, and the tide was low. The tug *Hellevoetsilius* lowered a boat manned by pilots' apprentices. Watched by spectators ashore they made repeated attempts to get a line over to the Berlin. One of the rescuers eventually managed to seize the end of a boat's fall which was hanging down from the Berlin*'s* side. Communication with the wreck had at length been established. 8 survivors were to slide down this to safety, three women were left aboard, too exhausted with cold and fatigue to rescue themselves. These were eventually rescued by the tug *Wodan*. There were no further survivors of the wreck, and although the death toll was never finally established the subsequent Board of Enquiry found that in its opinion 85 passengers and 48 of the crew, including all the certificated officers, were lost. At the time, the loss of so many lives made this the worst peacetime disaster in North Sea passenger travel.

(Hadfield, R. L., Sea Toll Of Our Time)
(Read more at wrecksite: https://www.wrecksite.eu/wreck.aspx?652)

During a debate in Parliament in 1912 on the loss of life at sea, Conservative M.P. Thomas Sandys, raised the example of the Berlin.

> "Take exactly what happened in the case of the "Berlin," and the result of the investigation which was conducted into that wreck. It was made clear to anyone who read the account of that disaster that the loss of life which occurred on that occasion was entirely attributable to the absence of effective line-throwing apparatus on board. If there had been a proper apparatus on board, there is no question that every person on board that ship would have been saved."

Following an Inquiry into the sinking, recommendations had been made that apparatus of this kind should be provided on all British ships in the future. Then the process of shifting responsibility began. The former serving Army Officer, now a Member of Parliament. continued;

"The matter was referred by the Board of Trade to the Merchant Shipping Advisory Committee, who reconsidered the whole matter, and came to no decision at all, except to refer the matter to a special Sub-committee. These appliances were tested all over the Kingdom at considerable cost to the British taxpayer. The Sub-committee, in the course of their investigations, visited the Mersey and the Tyne, then went to Dundee, and they finally wound up their travels in London. It would be interesting to know what the expense of this investigation was, because the Committee appear to have made an almost complete tour of Great Britain, and when they had completed their investigation, they came to the decision to send the matter back to the Merchant Shipping Advisory Committee to reconsider the whole question anew."

By this time, a considerable amount of time had elapsed. Then the Merchant Shipping Advisory Committee issued a Report to the Board of Trade, urging the necessity for the further provision of some form of line-throwing apparatus on board all British ships. Then, of course, the whole thing completely fizzled out. Sandys explained that the Board of Trade issued a circular "of an extremely anaemic character," in which they endorsed the recommendations of the Committee to the attention of those concerned but regretted that they had no powers in the matter whatever.

There the whole matter ended, Sandys concluded, and so far, as he was aware no provision was made to "carry out the recommendations which were made at the Board of

Trade inquiry into the circumstances which attended the wreck of the "Berlin."

(Board Of Trade—Loss Of Life At Sea. HC Deb 21 May 1912 vol 38 cc1790)

In a damning indictment of the whole sorry business Thomas Sandys asked inquiringly;

"The Board of Trade are continually finding an excuse for their inefficiency by stating that they have no power to act. That was their excuse with reference to this particular case. (Berlin) Have they ever applied here for powers to act in order to protect travellers and for the greater safety of our ships, and have those powers ever been refused to them? Do they ever seek such powers and find themselves unable to obtain them. The only object they have always had in view has been to satisfy public opinion for the time, and then, with their usual incorrigible slackness, to let things drift on as they were before."

(Board Of Trade—Loss Of Life At Sea. HC Deb 21 May 1912 vol 38 cc1791)

Needless to say, he never received an answer.

Fast forward to 1908, the subject of formal investigations into shipping losses was raised again, this time in the House of Lords by another advocate of seamen's safety.

Lord Muskery rose before the House;

"To call attention to the fact that the Board of Trade have not ordered formal investigations into the circumstances attending the losses of the missing steamers "Neptune" and "Grindon Hall"; to ask the reason, or reasons, for this; whether a preliminary inquiry has been held in regard to the

"Neptune," and, if so, by whom; and why, in the case of the "Grindon Hall," a preliminary inquiry was conducted in private by the Cardiff Stipendiary, assisted by a nautical assessor, instead of, as usual, by the Collector of Customs: also, to move that, in the opinion of this House, it is desirable that in every case where a British ship is posted as missing and given up as lost, a public investigation should, when practicable, be ordered by the Board of Trade in order, if possible, to elicit any material facts which might tend to throw light on the probable cause of the disaster."

(Missing British Ships. HL Deb 06 July 1908 vol 191 cc1149-63)

During the Inquiry, the Attorney-General had begun his questioning of Howell by asking "*the number of passengers who lost their lives over a period of years on voyages from the United Kingdom to America.*" However, during this early phase of questioning, the witness is repeatedly asked, for confirmation of figures pertaining to vessels "*belonging to the United Kingdom.*" There appears to be some misunderstanding between the Attorney-General and the witness, before Sir Rufus Isaacs corrected himself by acknowledging the figures as being all vessels, foreign and British, Sir Walter Howell had gone along with the error. However, it suggests, as Sir Rufus Isaacs repeated the request no fewer than six times, the Attorney-General wanted the Court to hear the witness state figures implying they were only for vessels, "*belonging to the U.K.*"

The tables on page 264 of the briefing documents, referred to by Sir Walter Howell, speak of "*the number of passengers*

embarked in the United Kingdom for ports in the United States or British North America and the number of passengers landed in the United Kingdom from the United States or British North America."
(Authors Italics)

As mentioned previously, it was not uncommon for many British shipping lines to commence their Trans-Atlantic trips from ports in the Mediterranean and Adriatic, as well as North Sea ports. Although some emigrants did make their way to the U.K. for embarkation at British ports as the rail fares and ferry charges to the U.K. were often cheaper than the cost of the sea passage from Europe to the U.K.

The significance lies in the Attorney-General's first question, which concluded by stating;

"*The point of it is that the Court may have before it what did happen during the 20 years that preceded this accident, and it has a material bearing of course upon the recommendations that ought to have been made and that were made.*" (Authors Italics)

We would come to know the precision with which the Attorney-General's questioning at times would elicit responses from witnesses and the care taken in the wording of his questions. Was this a notable instance of bureaucratic 'sleight of hand' in operation, which appears to exclude or diminish 'unfavourable' casualties from the figures, thereby minimising the numbers of actual losses?

That the Attorney-General, was presumably, reading from the same briefing notes as Sir Walter Howell is evident; however, Lord Mersey remains unusually silent during this testimony. As only one reference is made, "*as your Lordship sees*," from that, we cannot conclude that Lord Mersey has a copy of the figures before him. We are left to assume two possible scenarios, that Lord Mersey was following the exchange and the notes himself or was, uncharacteristically, content to sit and listen to testimony without notes. No mention is made of a copy of the notes being handed in. This is inconsistent with other areas of the Inquiry, where reference to which page the information could be found was made for Lord Mersey's convenience. Finally, as was said previously, no mention is made of the tables in Lord Mersey's Final Report.

Were the contents of the tables so negative to the Board of Trades' defence of past inactions as to warrant departmental deceit? The answer is complex; the tables in the briefing note only show what was in the 'script' for witnesses and inquisitors to follow.

There were only two members of counsel who asked the witnesses questions, Mr Butler-Aspinall for the Board of Trade and the Attorney-General. A strange reversal of roles as Sir Walter Howell was an employee of the Board of Trade, and Sir Norman Hill was there in his capacity as Chairman of the Board of Trade's Advisory Group. The questioning of Sir Walter Howell can be interpreted as the Attorney-General wanting to carefully guide the direction of his testimony. The more mundane and narrow the scope of the briefing notes about shipping losses, the less scrutiny there would be over any irregularities. If we were to conclude that Sir Walter Howell was being led by the hand, figuratively speaking, through this part of his testimony would not be surprising as we shall discover in other aspects of Sir Walter Howell's evidence that he avoided answering technical questions directly and seemed anxious to be put on the spot, much to the collective irritation of the Court. Secondly, suppose it should become known that shipping, in general, carried a greater risk and larger loss of life, and Trans-Atlantic shipping particularly was not, in fact, "*immune from lo*ss." In that case, the Court may have concluded that risks were being taken in full knowledge of the dangers, in this case, placing the White Star Line in an invidious position that a verdict of culpability against the company could have put her future enterprise as a shipping line in jeopardy. High stakes were being gambled.

We remind ourselves, the Attorney-General had asked earlier.

"*Will you give me the number of passengers who during that period of ten years lost their lives by casualties to vessels belonging to the United Kingdom?*"

Howell had stated;

"*In the years 1892 to 1901, the number of passengers lost by casualties to vessels at sea was - west-bound 66, eastbound 7. Seventy-three in all? - Seventy-three in all he confirmed. Have you also considered the figures for the ten years 1902 to 1911? - Yes. - west-bound 8, eastbound 1. - Nine in all during that ten years? - Nine in all.*"

(Brit Inq 22141-151)

As we will see, there were many other notable losses, not always with loss of life to passengers.

On November 20, 1898, the Jarrow-built SS *Principia* of the Arrow Shipping Co, outward bound from Dundee to New York with a general cargo, caught fire 140 miles off Cape

Wrath. The vessel ran for the Faroe Islands but struck rocks and sank, whereupon 27 crewmen and the sole passenger lost their lives. Only one crew member survived.
An example whereby limiting the calculations to incidents only within the narrow band of eleven years and only where more than 50 lives were lost; the official tables distort the true figures.
The Board of Trade's Table 2 for 1898 refers to 45 passengers going west and two passengers travelling east as having lost their lives. The lives of officers and crew did not merit a mention.
For the period cited by the Attorney-General, 1902-1911, Lloyd's Register of British and Foreign Shipping notes that during that period, there were around 45 notable incidents involving vessels that came to a mishap. Of these, 28 involved losses of life. Lloyds includes only vessels over 100 tons and does not routinely record loss of life. These 45 vessels have been taken from Lloyd's list as a sample only include those over 1,000 grt, i.e., those more capable of ocean crossings and large enough to accommodate passengers. Of the 28 where it is believed life was lost, but accurate figures are difficult to confirm, there were roughly 757 deaths from one cause or another; some losses, such as those from the *Republic*, were mercifully few; others were counted in the hundreds. Losses occurred in British and foreign vessels, passengers, and crew, in all seaways, across many oceans. during the 1871-1911 period.
(Lloyds Register of British And Foreign Shipping, 1890-1912)

In total, a conservative estimate of 6,789 lives could be accounted for as having been lost at sea from one catastrophe or another during the 1871-1911 period.

Both the Board of Trade and the shipping lines had their reasons for maintaining the Trans-Atlantic status quo and avoiding reactionary impositions on the rebound of a public inquiry.

Many smaller cargo vessels carried fare-paying passengers. The shipping lines eager to exploit every opportunity to make a profit. Also, the cost to travellers taking passage on a cargo freighter was often much less, making it more attractive for emigrants with less financial means. However, not subject to the same inspections, facilities onboard could be basic. Ships' passenger manifests were often informally recorded, and when such a vessel foundered, numbers lost could be vague. Ironically, proportionately, lifeboat provision on these passenger-carrying cargo vessels was much greater than on the larger passenger steamers. Nominally, enough lifeboat capacity for all on board on each side of the vessel. Stowaways, for instance, not only ran the risk of being discovered but also of becoming victims themselves. The Board of Trade tables (pages 304-331) record that no less than 18 stowaways were discovered when the vessels got into difficulty; of these, two who had stolen aboard ended up paying the ultimate price and lost their lives.

The first decade of the 20th century was fortuitous for ocean travel as there were fewer casualties than in previous decades. The year 1907 saw the peak of emigration to the U.S., and while it is true there were fewer casualties, they still occurred. In addition to those mentioned previously, incidents of note include January 9, 1903, the Elder Dempster steamer, *Palmas*, went missing on a voyage between Newport and Boston with the loss of 39 lives.

In March 1906, the lives of 28 were taken when the S.S. *British King* sank in the Atlantic en route from New York to Antwerp. The following year, 1908 saw another British vessel, *St Cuthbert*, bound for New York, catch fire, causing the death of 15 of her crewmen. It was not only British vessels that came to grief when in October, but French-owned *Neustria* also went missing somewhere in the Atlantic on a voyage from New York to Marseilles with the loss of 38 onboard.

Another example would be the case of the S.S. *Waratah*, a British-registered passenger and cargo vessel built on the Clyde in 1908 for the Blue Anchor Line to operate between Europe and Australia. On only her second voyage, in July 1909, the ship, during its passage from Durban to Cape Town, disappeared in mysterious circumstances with 211 passengers and crew aboard. Dubbed "Australia's Titanic," the vessel had many of the same design features as the ill-fated *Titanic*; her Captain, Josiah Ilbury, was well-regarded with a 40-year career at sea and even bore a striking resemblance to Captain E.J. Smith of *Titanic* notoriety.

(Further reading; The Lost Ship SS "Waratah" P.J. Smith. 2009)

Towards the end of the decade, the Donaldson Line's S.S. *Hestia* was lost on October 25, 1909, with 35 crew and five passengers on board, all of whom drowned when she was wrecked on Grand Manan Island in the Bay of Fundy. Six of the crew survived to tell their harrowing tale of having to

cling to the ship rigging before being rescued. The discovery of the ship's plight from the shore was delayed by thick weather. The survivors were lashed to the rigging for thirty-eight hours without either food or water, and when they were taken off by the lifeboat their condition was pitiable. After they had been in the rigging for twenty-four hours there were indications that caused them to fear that the mast would fall, and they therefore changed their position, working their way slowly and cautiously to the bridge, which was still out of water. It was, however, so exposed to the seas breaking over the vessel that they were obliged to return to the rigging. It is supposed that the vessel was misled by a wrong light, with the result that she was carried miles out of her course. All the crew were shipped at Glasgow and were chiefly Clyde men. The four Glasgow boys reported drowned were on their way to Canada in charge of horses with which to start farming.
(wrecksite.eu)
(Dictionary of Disasters at Sea During the Age of Steam: 1824-1962, Vol 1 A-L. Charles Hocking, 1969)

The SOS distress call was believed to have been used for the first time on 10 June 1909 when the Cunard liner *Slavonia* transmitted the signal after fatally running aground off the Azores. The message was received by the nearby NDL liner *Princess Irene*, which joined the effort to save the stricken vessel's passengers and crew. Nearby Cunard sister ship, *Batavia*, spotting a visual distress signal from *Slavonia*, also raced to the scene.

In 1904, *Slavonia* previously made history by transmitting, the first personal telegraph message ever sent from a ship at sea to a land station. A birthday greeting to Emperor

Franz Josef of Austria-Hungary was sent at the request of Hungarian members of the Hague Peace Commission. The message was transmitted by Medora Olive Newell, an experienced telegrapher who was a passenger on the liner. Newell may also have been the first woman to operate a shipboard wireless station.

In warmer climes, the *Fifeshire* mentioned previously, left Melbourne toward the end of July 1911 for London with 36 passengers on board. The total, including passengers and crew on board when she left for her destination, was 105. On the night of August 9, the liner was 20 miles South of Cape Guardafui, near Aden, when at 10.30 p.m. in fine, hazy weather, she became stranded in shallow water. There was no loss of life as a result of the stranding, and the next day the captain sent one of the lifeboats under the first officer, with five seamen to obtain assistance. As luck would have it, this boat ran into a gale which swept her some 250 miles from the scene of the wreck, and she was picked up five days later by the S.S. *Ardandearg* with her occupants at the point of exhaustion. Meanwhile, the position of the *Fifeshire* was becoming more precarious as the seas were pounding onto her. The order was given to abandon ship, and four boats under the captain, second, third and fourth officers, respectively, were got away with all the remaining people on board. The last boat left at noon on the 11th, and during daylight, they managed to keep close to each other. The next morning, however, the Captain's boat was alone, the second officer's boat, which had been nearest, had disappeared during the night, and the other boats had been picked up by the French liner *Adour*.

Later the same vessel picked up the captain's boat, but the second officer's boat could not be located. The number missing was 24, of whom ten were passengers.

(Dictionary of Disasters at Sea During the Age of Steam: 1824-1962, Vol 1 A-L. Charles Hocking, 1969)

Before the year was out, in November, the Norwegian steamer *Stikelstad*, owned by Klaverness and built by Doxford and Sons in Sunderland, went missing on a voyage from Glasgow to Melbourne, taking the lives of all 22 crewmen. May 1911 saw the demise of the Shire Line's S.S. *Gulf Stream* bound for Vancouver from Glasgow. Somewhere in the vast Atlantic, 25 lives were lost when she went missing. In that brief description of sinkings and disappearances, there were over 480 lives lost.

The list is not exhaustive; the details are often sketchy and incomplete, lives lost were not always scrupulously recorded, and passenger and crew manifests could be inaccurate. Shipping lines did not advertise losses at sea.

The issue remained that this part of the British Inquiry was being led by questions which elicited only figures of losses from passenger vessels and only those in the North Atlantic; even though smaller in number, many fare-paying emigrants could only afford tickets on cheaper, slower passenger-carrying cargo vessels, often, in some cases, sharing their voyage with livestock, although mercifully, not in the same space. Comfort came at a premium. As if to morbidly celebrate the seemingly low figures submitted by the Board of Trade, the Attorney-General asked the witness:

"You told me that by far the larger proportion of passengers included in the total of six million was carried in vessels belonging to the United Kingdom? - Yes." The Commissioner added: "The total loss comes to about four persons in a year. That is counting the twenty years." The Attorney-General offered: "Yes. Taking the whole 20 years it is about four a year."
(Brit Inq 22154)

Any doubts that were lingering about Lord Mersey's awareness of the figures were answered. One could be cynical and almost imagine the token back-slapping taking place among the representatives of the Board of Trade as if a great achievement had been made.

The period 1901-11, according to Sir Walter Howell, involved only one incident where the loss of life exceeded 50, the *Huronian* in February 1902. Although casualties totalling 757 souls were lost from vessels and losses documented by Lloyd's for the same period, some of those were also noted by the Board of Trade but not included in Sir Walter's list.

Of course, if you only include British passenger vessels where over 50 lives were lost in the North Atlantic, you dismiss the tragic ending to the Danish vessel S.S. *Norge*, which in 1904 ran aground off Rockall and 620 lives were lost; however, as she was not a 'British' vessel, she too would be excluded, even though she was built on the Clyde by Alexander Stephens of Govan and also subject to the same regulations of design and construction.

The Attorney-General continued;

"But in this later table of the forty years which you have given, that only deals with casualties in which over fifty lives were lost. Is that right? - That is quite right."

A brutal and harsh example of Board of Trade obfuscation, if ever there was. Again, why include only casualties with over 50 losses of life? No explanation was asked or forthcoming.

Interestingly, in their summations, no one, not Lord Mersey, none of the other counsel, assessors or seaman's representatives would comment on the obvious discrepancies in the numbers that were given by both Board of Trade "experts." Just how important is the accuracy of these losses? Well, the various Board of Trade advisory committees presumably, using these same data, claimed they based their entire shipping strategies on the alleged relatively safe record of Trans-Atlantic crossings and used that to justify many of their actions in the period preceding the *Titanic* sinking. Proof, if such was needed, came during Sir Walter Howell's testimony when the subject of revision of the Rules relating to the provision of lifeboats was raised by the Attorney-General;

"You see what I am directing attention to? - Yes, the period in 1904. I know the attention of the professional Officer was specially directed to that subject at that time, and as far as I remember, what he said to me as the result of conversations was that he was strongly of opinion that the increase of tonnage and accompanying increase of persons carried "was counterbalanced by the greater safety of the ships themselves." This greater safety I understood was due, first, to improvements of construction; second, the adoption of regular routes across the Atlantic to avoid collisions with other vessels and avoiding ice; and third, somewhat later, the introduction of wireless telegraphy."

Clearly, the Attorney-General was promoting the measures introduced by the Board of Trade. He continued;

"Let us pause there for a moment. That means, when this question was considered, there were those three factors to be taken into account. When you speak of improved construction, does that take into account and cover also the subdivision into watertight compartments? - That is the main point of it, I think."

Some shameless prompting of the witness was evident. No cries of objection my Lord! were heard as this was not a proper Court of Law. The dialogue continued;

"Then there was further this, that regular routes had been adopted across the North Atlantic out and home? - Quite. Which gave greater safety? - As I understand it, they were laid down for that purpose. To avoid collisions? - Yes, avoiding collisions with other vessels and with ice. Then there is the third element which was taken into consideration, and that was the introduction of wireless telegraphy? - Quite; I understood that those were the main reasons which influenced him. Which, of course, gave an opportunity of calling for assistance? - Yes."
(Brit Inq 22410-417)

A petulant Attorney-General had interrupted the questioning by Mr Dunlap, counsel for the Leyland Line, during his questioning of Stanley Lord:

> "*I do not quite know what this is leading to. My friend is supposing to be cross-examining this Witness. If not, I think it would be better to allow him to tell his story himself. I do not quite appreciate what my friend's position is. I quite understand that he is here for the protection of the Master, and I am raising no objection to that, but in all the circumstances I think it would be better to let him tell a little of the story.*
> Mr Dunlop: *I am coming to the part I want him to speak about.*
> The Commissioner: *I do not think any harm has been done.*
> The Attorney-General: *I am only intervening so that it may not be done later.*" (Authors Italics)
> (Brit Inq 7355)

The old proverb 'What's sauce for the goose is sauce for the gander' applies in this case.

Some would later point an accusatory finger at the Attorney-General's embroilment in the Marconi debacle. Sir Rufus would have done well to remember Shakespeare's Hamlet when he too was 'hoist by his own petard'.

An editorial which appeared in the June 19, 1913, edition of the Times when the "Marconi shares affair" was still raw, stated:

> "A man is not blamed for being splashed with mud. He is commiserated. But if he has stepped into a puddle which he might easily have avoided, we say that it is his own fault. If he protests that he did not know it was a puddle, we say that he ought to know

better; but if he says that it was after all quite a clean puddle, then we judge him deficient in the sense of cleanliness. And the British public like their public men to have a very nice sense of cleanliness."

Sir Rufus had fallen foul of the very behaviour he cautioned others against.

In the space of two paragraphs, Sir Walter conveniently mentions ice and the conscientious measures the Board of Trade took to avoid colliding with it and throwing the responsibility for the sinking back onto the hapless ship's Captain.

Continuing to prise every ounce of leverage from the statement, the Attorney-General asked Sir Walter Howell another leading question;

"Then, was any consideration directed to the number of disasters in the trans-Atlantic passenger trade? – Oh, yes. I remember the splendid record of safety of life at sea was one of the points to which attention was directed then."

(Brit Inq 22410-17)

Like a well-rehearsed Edwardian music hall double act, Sir Walter Howell was again obediently taking his cue from Sir Rufus Isaacs, notably without intervention from Lord Mersey.

The Attorney-General went on;

"The (shipping) figures which you gave me yesterday have shown us what, in fact, were the casualties which had occurred during the years 1892 to 1901, and I suppose that could have been ascertained up to 1904, or very nearly to 1904? -

Oh, yes. All those matters were taken into consideration? - Yes, I am quite sure they were. And as a consequence, no alteration was made? - Yes, that is so."

(Brit Inq 22419-20)

Confirmation that policy as far back as 1904 was being led by Howell's so-called "*splendid record of safety*," was shamelessly, validated by the country's senior law official.

The subject of wireless telegraphy in merchant ships received some attention in Parliament during the final few years leading up to the loss of the *Titanic*. The discussion at the core of these questions was that the Board of Trade should make it compulsory for certain classes of vessels (especially ocean-going passenger vessels) to be fitted with wireless apparatus. This suggestion was probably inspired by the fact that the use of wireless telegraphy in connection with some significant shipping casualties had received widespread press coverage and excited great public interest.

The Board of Trade had no powers under the law as it stood then to compel passenger ships to carry wireless apparatus; the reason given was that wireless telegraphy could not be included in the requirements issued under section 418 of the Merchant Shipping Act, 1894, which deals with lights, fog-signals, and the rule of the road at sea, nor was it regarded as a life-saving appliance within the meaning of section 427. To make the fitting of wireless telegraphy compulsory on any class of ships required the legislation to be changed. We recall how Sir Alfred Chalmers had included the availability of wireless telegraphy as a feature that improved the safety of vessels at sea and one of the reasons given why there were so few losses. Just exactly how Sir Alfred Chalmers could make such a claim was beyond understanding as those minority of ships able to send and receive messages back and forth regarding weather conditions for example, was amply demonstrated in *Titanic*'s case that some of these same messages were forgotten or ignored for the purpose for which they were sent. In contrast, the views of some M.P.'s were quite vociferous in their opposition to its introduction.

In July 1910, M.P. for Hythe, Sir Edward Sassoon introduced a Bill into the House of Commons to make wireless telegraphy compulsory on ocean-going vessels carrying 50 or more persons (including passengers and crew) from a British port, citing the recent examples of the *City of Paris*, *St. Louis*, and the *Republic*. In a passionate appeal, he pleaded;

"This invention is marvellous and subtle almost beyond anything that human ingenuity has yet devised. It has thoroughly established its claims to serious consideration by the phenomenal manifestations of its use in so many recent instances where, but for its powerful aid, the world would have had to mourn the loss of many valuable lives."

Sir Edward Sassoon was naive if he believed that ship owners would willingly embrace any technology that cost money, however beneficial its function, at least until they discovered that wealthier passengers would pay money to send frivolous messages back and forth to the mainland. A practice which would indeed prove costly to the *Titanic*. His

timing was premature in the development of a workable system of land-based stations. Speaking in opposition to the proposed Bill was Conservative M.P. for King's Lynn, Edward Gibson Bowles, perhaps better known to history as the founder of the society magazine *Vanity Fair* and *The Lady*, still in print in the present day. He was not to pull his punches. Describing the Bill as "*well-meant*," he then went on to say, "There is great danger of its doing far more harm than good to those whom it is intended to benefit."
Pointing out; "that large passenger vessels have already largely provided themselves with wireless telegraphy, and that the others do not need it."

"If this Bill were passed, he said, if there were imposed upon every passenger, or other ship, or any ship, the obligation to install a system of wireless telegraphy, first of all there is the question of the expense of the system, and secondly there is the expense of carrying a man. I think indeed you can hardly do with less than two extra men, for one man could not be on duty day and night."

He then went on;

"My objection goes further. To apply these requirements to our shipping would place it at a very great disadvantage with foreign shipping and would mean putting our shipping under further harassing regulations of the Board of Trade, which has never done anything but mischief to the shipping trade. It has ruined many of the shipowners, and it has in no way improved the shipping of this country. In the interests of shipping all the officials of the Board of Trade should be strangled or marooned on a desert island, so that they might leave shipping alone. They have been a great curse to the shipping trade, and now the hon. Baronet proposes to institute a further set of regulations to be carried out by the same Board of Trade which has already oppressed the shipping of this country as much as it possibly can."

Underlying his vitriol towards the Board of Trade, he did make some telling points.

"It is no use to install wireless telegraphy on board a ship unless you have stations on land to take in the messages. In Europe and between here and New York there are many stations, and they are under the control of the Post Office; but, like everything under the control of a public Department, they are hundreds of years behind the times. They are so bad as to be almost useless, and there is no possible hope of expectation of improvement."

Therefore, he continued, "I do not think the hon. Baronet has made out a case. I think his Bill would increase the tyrannical powers of the Board of Trade, and it would largely add to the expenses of owners of passenger ships. It would impose upon them the need for carrying this wireless telegraphy, which itself is only in its early stage."

Despite his tenacious criticism, he did not appear to have any ties to ship owners or the industry in general.

He was, however, backed by some impressive support in the form of fellow Conservative M.P. Lieut-Colonel Walter Guinness, whose great-great-grandfather Arthur Guinness founded the brewing empire, which bears his name. In 1912, the magazine, *The Outlook*, owned by the Guinness family, broke the news of the "Marconi Scandal" by accusing, among others, Chancellor of the Exchequer, Lloyd George and notably Attorney-General Sir Rufus Isaacs of share fraud about the time of the Inquiry. He concluded his speech by stating;

> "The time is not ripe for this Bill; the Board of Trade is not to be trusted; and I hope this Bill if leave is given to introduce it, will be allowed to proceed no further than its First Reading."

The Bill was not proceeded with.

(Wireless Telegraph Installation (Passenger Ships). HC Deb July 13, 1910, Vol 19 Cc381-6)

In what might be viewed as predictable civil service behaviour, the whole subject had been attentively watched by the Board of Trade in conjunction with the other Departments concerned, and the question of compulsion had been "carefully considered" on several occasions. An Inter-Departmental Committee on Wireless Telegraphy reported against compulsion in March 1909, and their view was adopted by the Board of Trade, who maintained that view up to the sinking of the *Titanic* after which, of course, everything changed.

The main reason, as far as the Board of Trade were concerned, was that, in view of the rapidity with which wireless telegraphy had been adopted voluntarily by British shipowners, compulsion would have been premature, for the government believed it was obviously better to allow shipowners the opportunity of fitting the apparatus on their own account, and in a manner and at a time which is convenient to them, than to pass legislation, which may prove irksome to both the enterprising and unenterprising firms at the same time. A feature of the Board of Trade's laissez-faire attitudes that permeated the late nineteenth and early twentieth-century policymaking.

The progress that had been made up to the *Titanic* sinking in equipping British ships with wireless telegraphy reveals that over half the total number of foreign-going passenger steamers were already fitted and about one-tenth of the number of steamers holding home-trade passenger certificates. Some routes were not well equipped with land wireless stations, and as the number of land stations on these routes increased, the vessels using the routes would be more generally equipped than they were. The British Inquiry would unearth the inherent weaknesses in the operation of wireless telegraphy when it was left up to the shipping lines who did not employ the Marconi operators on board ships and certain ships captains, including possibly, Captain Stanley Lord of the *Californian*, who did not embrace the new technology to its full potential.

The *Titanic* disaster resuscitated interest in the use of wireless telegraphy as an aid to the safety of shipping and directed special attention to the question of the number of operators carried and the importance of arrangements being made to allow for a continuous service being maintained at the apparatus, so that distress signals sent out by other ships may be certain of being given attention. The question of wireless telegraphy was referred to the Merchant Shipping Advisory Committee, which, not surprisingly, appointed a sub-committee to consider it containing representatives of the Board of Trade and the General Post Office.

The *Titanic* Inquiry would discover that up to the date of the publication of the last supplement (April 15, 1912), 410 such vessels were fitted with wireless. Of these, 283 vessels held foreign-going passenger certificates issued by the Board of Trade, 31 held home-trade certificates, and 96 held no certificates. It may be added, for the purposes of comparison, that the total number of steamers holding foreign-going passenger certificates issued by the Board of Trade is about 530, and the total number of those holding home-trade certificates is about 320.

The following table shows the progress which had been made in equipping British ships with wireless telegraphy and that the average rate of increase for the last year was 11 each month.

Number fitted at the end of:

1909 - 116
1910 - 170
1911 - 275
1912 - 410
(MT9/920F Pages 361-2)

The loss of the *Titanic* would highlight the need for the adoption of a universal system and agreement between nations on the use of wireless telegraphy and, not least, the need to guarantee the privacy of communication.

The regulations in the 1894 Merchant Shipping Act and the extraordinary powers granted by the 1906 amendments given to the Board of Trade applied to all British registered vessels, not only those on the North Atlantic routes.

If the shipping figures the Board of Trade based their decisions on were inaccurate or false, then there was clear evidence of malfeasance as to the facts. The path to the endorsement of the giant 'Olympic-class' vessels with their capacious accommodations and their casual regulatory approval was strewn with the souls of hundreds lost at sea, passengers, and crewmen alike, including those in 'minor' shipping casualties where less than 50 lives were lost and evidently, were not to be mentioned in the Inquiry records and forgotten, in the intervening years.

As though he were *dramatis personae*, in some twisted Arthurian production, the Attorney-General might have taken some satisfaction from his bogus achievement and felt like the Edwardian equivalent of St George that he had plunged the dagger of deception into the heart of the beast of truth as it thrashed its final death throes on the floor of the Scottish Drill Hall.

Was this confirmation that those Mediterranean, Adriatic and North Sea ports of departure for passenger vessels carrying emigrants to North American destinations were not included in the calculations for shipping losses? Even though, as we have seen, many British operators chose to commence their outward-bound voyages from places other than the U.K. Did they do this also as a way of avoiding inspections on their arrival at UK ports?

Only when it came to the Final Arguments would the alleged "*safe*" record of Trans-Atlantic seafaring be raised again, unchallenged, almost triumphantly, by counsel for the White Star Line.

What is less well known is that this was not the first time Sir Walter Howell could be accused of deception. Lord Muskerry, a constant thorn in the side of the Board of Trade, raised a question in Parliament in December 1912 concerning the Marine Department of The Board of Trade;

"That in the opinion of this House an inquiry should be held into the constitution and administration of the Marine Department of the Board of Trade in the interest of safety of life at sea and the welfare and efficiency of our mercantile marine."

He went on;

"In the year 1903, this House agreed that a Select Committee* should be appointed to investigate the dangers incurred through ships being allowed to go to sea with insufficient ballast. In support of my case—that many lives had been sacrificed at sea owing to insufficiently ballasted ships—amongst those witnesses expressing themselves in the strongest way were nautical assessors, who are appointed by the Home Office to sit on Courts of Inquiry in connection with disasters to ships occurring in the mercantile marine. They are not appointed by the Board of Trade; therefore, we can look upon them as thoroughly independent witnesses. Amongst others to support me were merchant shipmasters, underwriters, naval architects, marine engineers, and other expert witnesses, all of whom were in absolute accord as to the necessity of a light load line."

The damaging declaration followed;

"To my profound astonishment, I found that the chief and most strenuous witness in the way of opposition was the Assistant Secretary at the head of the Marine Department of the Board of Trade, still occupies this position. In the course of his evidence, he produced a number of figures which greatly impressed the Select Committee, who quite accepted them. A subsequent searching analysis of these figures both on my part and that of the Imperial Merchant Service Guild, on whose behalf I was working, showed that these figures had manifestly been "cooked" so as to mislead in order to bolster up the case against the Light Load Line Bill. The Board of Trade were very naturally supported by certain of the shipowners, and thus you will see how the endeavours to ensure greater safety of life at sea were frustrated by the Marine Department of the Board of Trade."

*(Report From The Select Committee Of The House Of Lords On Light Load Line With Proceedings Of The Committee Session 1903) (MT9/920H)

"Surely, the Earl of Granard asked, "the noble Lord does not believe that an efficient and reliable Civil Servant would sink to the depth of "cooking" figures for a Return such as that."

"Yes," was the emphatic reply from Lord Muskerry.

(HL Deb December 09, 1912, vol 13 cc90-104)

Of course, at that time, Lord Muskerry was invoking Parliamentary privilege to make an accusation of impropriety in office.

The Journal of Commerce wrote on December 11, 1912;
> "The Earl of Granard, in speaking on behalf of the Government, did not show any very intimate acquaintanceship with the subject, and the way in which Captain Chalmers, one of the best nautical men who has ever been seen at the Board of Trade, was thrown over by the Department, and the whole blame for the policy adopted with regard to boats placed on his shoulders, was anything but edifying."

The article went on;
> "Lord Muskerry had based his demand on the interests of the safety of life at sea, and, as Lord Salisbury cogently urged, the substance of the whole matter is that unless the Titanic disaster be taken to be a common occurrence, and not a wholly exceptional instance, there is no reason whatever for uneasiness, either at the number or nature of the maritime disasters that are taking place."

In conclusion the article stated;
> "Lord Muskerry talked as though the British shipping business was especially favoured in being free from legislative interference, but, as a sensible, well-informed man, he can no meaner this than he can hope to justify his hasty assertion that the Board of Trade "cooks" its returns."

(MT9/920H)

That Lord Muskerry drew the ire of the 'shipping press' regarding his comments should come as no surprise. It was only when he sought to take his fight to a wider readership that he 'rattled' the Board of Trade.

On December 27, the Shipping Gazette published in full, a letter from Lord Muskerry to the Editor, a copy of which was retained in the National Archives, accompanied with an internal Board of Trade memorandum proving the letter was seen by senior Marine Department officials and reached all the way to the desk of the President, Sydney Buxton.
(MT9/920H)

The handwritten cover-note bemoaned the publication of the letter sent by Lord Muskerry to the shipping press but appeared to be relieved that it "only appeared in two (shipping) papers." The scribe went on; "The charge of "cooking" figures is of course unfounded, but unless repeated in the House of Commons I doubt if we should take any notice. No competent person will believe it."

More damningly, the letter Lord Muskery wrote to the Editor also said;

"The loss of the Titanic only aroused public interest because it concerned a great number of passengers and was a disaster of colossal magnitude. But, in conjunction with the Imperial Service Guild, whose cordial and strenuous co-operation I have ever had, it has been my endeavour to ensure that those disasters of a similar category which happen to cargo vessels where the crews only lose their lives, should receive just as much consideration. When the Titanic was lost the figures showing the comparatively infinitesimal loss of life as regards passengers, which were so freely produced as proof of safety at sea, and in justification of the policy of the Board of Trade, were merely treated with derision, and as of no real importance or bearing in connection with this terrible disaster. Why should it be any different in the case of a merchant cargo ship sacrificed, shall we say, to a huge deckload, when 30 or 40 of our sailors are drowned and misery and poverty are brought into, perhaps, as many homes. It is not a case of being melodramatic; it is a grim fact."

(Shipping Gazette, Friday December 27, 1912.) (MT9/920H)

Included in the document were type-written comments, the author of which is likely Sir Walter Howell given his seniority. However, in response to certain passages in Lord Muskerry's letter it says;

"These figures were facts and were surely pertinent to the question of the safety of life in the North Atlantic passenger trade."

The next comment reveals;

"The loss of cargo ships receives as much attention from the Board of Trade as the loss of passenger ships. It is only natural that the public should be more interested in "a disaster of colossal magnitude" than in smaller disasters, but the Board of Trade do not control public interest in events."

Further on it states;

"It is, at least, questionable whether he (Muskerry) has furnished "distinct proof" of loss of life from "preventable causes" which the Board of Trade have the power to deal with."

Finally, appearing to hide behind the verdict of the Inquiry the annotations state;

"All this was carefully considered by Lord Mersey, who blamed the Board for not keeping the boat scale up to date but held that if the scale had been revised it was doubtful whether the result would have increased the numbers of lives saved from the "Titanic."

The responses to Lord Muskerry's letter demonstrate once again that Board of Trade officials sought refuge from blame by hiding behind flawed reasoning. That these officials believed in their responsibilities is not in doubt. However, it might be said, that their obstinate adherence to that belief closed their minds to constructive criticism from outside sources.

Notwithstanding Howell's service as Private Secretary to the then President of the Board of Trade, Michael Hicks-Beech and the dubiety of shipping figures spoken of during an after-dinner speech mentioned previously, if Lord Muskerry was correct, then Sir Walter Howell was already practised in deception and again, nine years later, stands accused, in this account, of manipulating statistics to suit his own and the ship owner's agenda. There was no evidence to the contrary in 1903 and subsequently in 1912 when the accusations had more veracity when confronted by Sir Walter Howell's own Board of Trade figures to judge him.

The suggestion of malfeasance or simple incompetence on the part of Sir Walter Howell could be further argued when the remainder of his testimony before Lord Mersey is viewed.

The oftentimes abstruse responses under questioning made by Walter Howell when he came before the British Inquiry into the sinking of the *Titanic* on June 11, Day 21, did not go unnoticed. William Pringle, Liberal MP for Northwest Lanarkshire, stated in Parliament;

> "I think the evidence taken before Lord Mersey's Inquiry showed that there was a lack of coordination and that the head of the Marine Department seemed to be unable to give independent advice upon any specific question; he was only able to refer the question to one of his subordinates who was responsible for the particular Department to which the inquiry related."

(HC Deb October 07, 1912, vol 42 cc32-148)

During the same Debate, Sir Basil Peto reminded the House that in fact there is no 'Board of Trade'. The Board of Trade, he said, is the President of the Board of Trade. The effective administration so far as marine matters are concerned, is that of the Assistant Secretary of the Marine Department.

In defence of the office of the Assistant Secretary, by definition, Sir Walter Howell, Sir Basil Peto did comment on the diversity of the responsibilities of the department;

"I can only say that those for whom I speak, the Imperial Merchant Guild, which represents over 50 per cent. of British officers and masters of British ships, do not find, and have told me they do not find, a sympathetic reception for grievances, if you term them grievances, or questions which required attention in connection with the merchant service. I do not think this is very much to be wondered at if you consider the enormous number of things which the Marine Department of the Board of Trade is supposed to administer."

The hon. Member who has just addressed the House (Pringle) said that in the Inquiry before Lord Mersey, it was found that the Permanent Secretary of the Marine Department (Howell) had frequently to refer to underlings for information on specific subjects. If he were supposed to be familiar with all these subjects I have enumerated, I am not surprised that he had from time to time to refer to someone who happened to be in charge of the particular subject which was being discussed.

(Mr Peto. Lord Mersey's Report. HC Deb 07 October 1912 vol 42 col 119.)

It was established early on in the Inquiry by the Attorney-General that the Marine Department of the Board of Trade was charged with the administration of the Merchant Shipping Act 1894, specifically, all matters relating to merchant shipping and seamen; therefore, there was much interest in the answers Sir Walter Howell would be expected to provide during testimony before Lord Mersey, that would go some way into explaining why there was seemingly out-of-date regulations in place at the time of the sinking.

That he could be viewed as the 'pantomime villain' in the context of the ineffectual role he played as Chief of the Marine Department of the Board of Trade can be justified by reminding ourselves that the word 'pantomime' means 'imitator of all.' During his testimony, Sir Walter Howell fulfilled that description handsomely.

The Board of Trade had come under serious criticism for the administration of the rules which governed so many aspects of the mercantile marine. We already know of the scathing comments about the Board of Trade made by U.S. Senator Alden Smith in his report to the Senate.

In his official report, Mersey attempted to address the tortuous path the legislation had taken by the various committees, the decision-making process seemingly mired in departmental inertia.

(British Wreck Commissioner's Inquiry Report; Board of Trade's Administration)

As far back as March 1886, it seemed, the Board of Trade appointed a Departmental Committee to inquire into the question of boats, rafts and lifesaving apparatus carried by seagoing merchant ships. Obviously, a contentious question as it was still being "carefully considered" in December 1911. The Report came to the alarming conclusion, among other things;

> "As regards boats for ocean-going steamers carrying large numbers of passengers, we think they would be of little use in saving life (although they may for a time prolong its existence) unless succour is at hand from other ships or from proximity to shore. It is

obvious that though boats may save life for the moment, they can but prolong its existence for a time equivalent to the quantity of stores and freshwater they can carry for each person on board. In the Atlantic, in winter, for instance, persons in boats would suffer greatly, and probably die of starvation or exposure unless their ship was lost in the track of other vessels, which would, we fear, probably not be the case, unless an ocean track is decided on both outward and homeward for all vessels crossing the Atlantic between the United Kingdom and the ports in North, America."

(C5013 page 4) Extracts from Report of The Departmental Committee of 1886 on Boats, &C.)

And added, with special reference to steam passenger vessels carrying emigrants across the Atlantic to ports on the east coast of North America, they said as follows:

"Considering the number of vessels employed in this trade, and the large number of passengers they carry and also taking into consideration the stormy character of the ocean they have to cross, and the thick and foggy weather encountered, we think this class is the most important of any, and we cannot pass over the fact that of late years this traffic has been carried on with remarkable immunity from loss of life."

(C5013 pages 6&7) Passenger Steam Vessels carrying Emigrants or others across the Atlantic to Ports on the East Coast of North America.)

This dismissive explanation, which lay behind the rationale for the lack of lifeboats on the *Titanic* is perhaps well summarised by the conclusions of that Report. A succession of high-ranking Board of Trade officials would find concealment in their tortuous presentation of figures attributed to losses at sea which gave justification to taking risks with the lives of passengers and crew on vessels crossing the Atlantic at full speed. Until now, their disingenuous testimonies were recorded for all time and filed away to be largely forgotten.

During his questioning of Sir Walter Howell, the Attorney-General firstly tried to establish historically, from the Act of 1854, the earliest pertinent Merchant Shipping statute, how it came to be that the scale was gross tonnage instead of the number of passengers. When asked, Sir Walter Howell claimed he could not recollect specifically, but he stated there had been a "slight scale" before 1890 when these present Rules were drafted and eventually adopted.

(Brit Inq 22292-306)

"Can you tell us at all why it was that the change was made? - It was felt to be a better indication of the size and power of the ship - gross tonnage rather than net tonnage. Can you also tell us why it was that the scale that was adopted was a tonnage scale and not a number of passengers scale? - You mean adopted by this Committee?"

"Yes. I want you to follow the question that I am putting to you because at first sight, at any rate, it does not seem to be clear why, when you are providing accommodation for the crew and the passengers on a ship, you should provide the boating accommodation according to tonnage

118

instead of the number of persons to be carried in the ship? - Quite so."

The Attorney-General's dialogue suggested a tone of vexation in his words;

"That is what I want you to tell us? - When the Board of Trade later came to the Committee it said they were to have regard to several considerations: First of all, the number of persons carried; secondly, how many boats they could carry consistently with not destroying the stability or seaworthy qualities of the ship, or unduly hampering her decks. Then the Committee proceeded to consider it on those terms, and the point was mentioned whether they should take the basis on this view. I think it was mentioned, but only to be rejected at once, I think. At any rate, they adopted the basis of gross tonnage because they thought they were instructed to divide the ships into divisions and classes, and that that was a clear indication that they were to take size as the basis of their consideration. If it had been intended that they were to take the number of persons on board as their basis they would not have been told to divide the ships into classes. There would have been no necessity to do anything of the sort."

Howell's convoluted depiction of the inner workings of the Advisory Committees leaves one with the impression of a group of self-serving egotists.

"Told by whom? - In the Reference to them by the Board of Trade. The Reference to the Board of Trade was that the ships should be divided into classes and the Board of Trade passed that on to the Committee that ships should be divided into classes."

The Commissioner interrupted;

"What classes? - That was precisely the question they had to settle. They came to the conclusion that it meant classes having regard to their size as indicated by gross tonnage. I do not understand that. Can you tell me what the classes were that they did divide it into? - Yes, certainly. What were they? - First of all, emigrant passenger ships."

"Those classes I understand? - And then on to other classes."

"Were there other classes? - Yes, the foreign-going passenger ships, and then the foreign-going cargo steamships and steamers; I am speaking from memory. Then, sailing ships engaged in carrying passengers, and so on. It was graded into classes, and those classes were based upon gross tonnage, as being the best indication of the size of the ships."

The reputation Lord Mersey was to cultivate for intolerance in professional witnesses who showed prevarication in their testimony during the proceedings was much in evidence and would come increasingly to the fore while Sir Walter Howell was on the stand.

"But you have not answered the question that was put to you by the Attorney-General, he said: Why was it that tonnage measurements were taken as the standard to go by, rather than the number of persons carried on the ship? - That I think I can indicate quite clearly again; I had endeavoured too already."

Possibly for the first time in his recent career, Sir Walter Howell was being asked to explain his actions. Something he was evidently unused to doing.

"But you have not succeeded in informing my mind about it? - If it had been intended - I do not care about what was intended, but I want to know why it was - what the reason was for taking tonnage as the standard instead of the number of people whose lives were to be saved by the life-saving appliances? - The Committee proceeded at once to consider whether they could do it on that basis."

"Oh, well, if they could not do it on that basis, that is an excellent reason? - Then they proceeded to divide it into these divisions by tonnage, as they found the other impracticable."

"Either you do not understand my question, or I am not sufficiently intelligent to understand your answer; I do not know which it is. I want to know why, when they were applying themselves to the question of how to provide for the safety of a number of lives, they excluded the number of lives from consideration and took into consideration only the tonnage of the ship? - I should be sorry to say that was the only thing they took into consideration, but it was the main consideration."

(Brit Inq 22292-306)

Lord Mersey declared;

"You speak at large, and in language that I do not understand. You say the same principle runs through all the classes. What is the principle that you are talking about? - I said that - No, do tell me so that I may understand your answer. What is the principle to which you have just referred when you said the same principle would run through all the classes? What is the principle? - The principle running through all the classes, as they are at present, is the principle of gross tonnage, of course."

With more than a hint of resignation, the Commissioner said:

"That does not get us any forwarder."

(Brit Inq 22329-30)

Even in the present day, decades later, this exchange reflects incredibly poorly on a senior member of the Board of Trade, and it would have been even worse for those in the Scottish Drill Hall who must have squirmed with discomfort at these wretched meanderings of an explanation from someone in such high authority. Lord Mersey was showing much greater tolerance to this witness than others. Possibly due to his ennobled position.

The Attorney-General spoke;

"I will tell you what it shows. If I may say so respectfully, what my Lord says is really the crux of the criticism to be directed to this scale? - I am quite aware of that, and that will be dealt with by the professional Officers."

The Attorney-General: "We want to understand it."

The Commissioner pursued the witness;
"You have not answered my question, you pushed it off onto somebody else, who is not in the witness box, and that is: Why, having thought it worthwhile to make one alteration in the course of four years, did it never occur to anybody in the next 18 years to make any alteration? – That is a question I am not competent to answer."
(Brit Inq 22380-88)

"But I am sure, Sir Walter, that you must have talked about it to somebody in the Board of Trade? - Oh, yes. Now, to whom did you talk? - I talked to the professional Officer of the Marine Department. (Sir Alfred Chalmers) And what explanation did he give? - He said that he did not think the scale required any further alteration. Why not? - I have not a very clear recollection of what his reasons were. I would rather he gave them in his own words. I should have thought it was so important that you would have had? - No, because conversations were taking place frequently on many things."

The discomfiture that Sir Walter Howell must have been experiencing at this point was evident. His ordeal was not over yet. Almost contemptuously, Lord Mersey offered him a way out.

"The gentleman is here, I understand, and you prefer to leave him to get out of the difficulty? - I prefer that the professional Officer should answer professional questions."

The Attorney-General asked,

"To whom are you referring? - To Sir Alfred Chalmers, the professional adviser of the Board of Trade then."

(Brit Inq 22380-88)

From these early exchanges, it would not be wrong to surmise that apparently, with such weak leadership, should anyone seek to impose their own will on the decisions being made by the Marine Department with Sir Walter Howell's feebleness in office then that door was left wide open to be exploited. The dominant presence of Sir Alfred Chalmers was constantly, it seemed, lurking in the background. Later in his testimony, Sir Walter Howell is asked by Mr Scanlan;

"Do you mean the requirements of the bulkheads Committee as applied to a ship like the "*Titanic*"? - That I must leave to be explained by the technical Officers."

(Brit Inq 22544)

Again, by his own hand, he is publicly demeaned. Even Lord Mersey was growing weary of the excuses;

"Oh, dear, dear me. I get into confusion when you push off the answer to somebody else who is not in the witness box? - It is simply because I am afraid of misleading you, My Lord."

(Brit Inq 22544)

Further on in his testimony;

"I suggest to you that it is reasonable, and I ask your view? - I do not care to express my view, My Lord unless you tell me to. This is the way I can answer your question, that I think it is a matter that

deserves very attentive consideration. That is my personal view, please."
(Brit Inq 22633-34)

Unashamed, the prevarication continued.

"Your Department is responsible for making regulations to ensure the safety of the passengers carried? - Yes, but in any case, I am sure you do not wish to misunderstand me. I am not expressing here today the view of the Board of Trade. I expressed that personal view to you because I thought it was only fair to you."
(Brit Inq 22633-34)

Again, Mr Scanlan continues the questioning;

"Who will exercise the responsibility as to deciding the relative importance of a suggestion of this sort which may lead to a fresh instruction? - I have told you the technical Officers would advise the Department."
(Brit Inq 22684)

Later, in reply to a question posed by Mr Edwards;

"What I am most anxious that the Court should understand is that I am not a technical Officer but an administrative Officer and that the whole of my administrative staff is at your disposal.

The Commissioner, I wish you would try when the question admits of an answer of "yes" or "no," to answer it by "yes" or "no." - Yes, My Lord, I always try to do that."
(Brit Inq 22710)

Further on, he tested Mr Clement Edwards's patience to its limit;

125

"I did not ask you that, Sir Walter. Do you mind, please, answering my questions in the form in which they are put? Any qualification you like to make you can make afterwards, of course. Is it not a fact that, under your regulations, if there are four bulkheads put in, then your particular surveyor may issue a declaration of seaworthiness so far at all events as bulkheads are concerned? - And so far as his personal responsibility is concerned, yes."

Continuing;

"Is it not a fact that you have among your surveyors a large number of persons who have had no special training apart from any experience they may have derived in their position in the Board of Trade in the testing of the character of bulkheads? - Every Surveyor, before his appointment is confirmed, has to pass an examination that satisfies the Chief Ships' Surveyor that he is."

Lord Mersey interrupted brusquely;

"I wish you would try when the question admits of an answer of "yes" or "no," to answer it by "yes" or "no." - Yes, My Lord, I always try to do that. If you will listen to the question, put to you again, you will see that it admits of one of those answers."

The Commissioner invited Mr Edwards to repeat his question. "Now put it again, Mr Edwards";

"Have you not in your employment as Surveyors a number of gentlemen who have had no practical experience and training in bulkheads except what they have derived in their experience as Surveyors to the Board of Trade? - If I am to say "yes" or "no," I think I will say "no."

Perhaps believing he had made a breakthrough Mr Edwards closed in;

"Then we may take it from you that every one of your surveyors has had experience of testing bulkheads apart altogether from their experience in the Board of Trade? - That is where it becomes so necessary for me to qualify what I say."

"I did not ask you not to qualify your answer, Sir Walter. Qualify it as you like? - A Surveyor is not allowed to make a declaration for a vessel upon the particular points with which he is entrusted, that is to say, hull, equipment and machinery, until he has satisfied the Board of Trade that he is fit to do it."

A seemingly exasperated Lord Mersey comments;

"That is a very general and beautifully vague answer. What test have you at the Board of Trade for the efficiency of your surveyors in this matter of bulkheads? - That the Officer has passed the Chief Ships' Surveyor. I really must ask you to ask the ship's surveyor any further questions on that when he is examined. I cannot carry it any further."

The inveterate civil servant was not the best advertisement for a Grammar school education of the period. The long list of honours bestowed upon him and the rise to a position of influence in the Board of Trade, coupled with the sorry apology of a testimony, demeaned the responsibility his time in office required and an indication of the apparent torpor that was endemic in the Marine Department. Meanwhile, Mr Edwards persisted;

> "Who is the gentleman that you suggest that I should ask because it seems in this Enquiry we are constantly being put off and told that other people are coming who will give the information, and when they come, they do not give it? Will you give me the name of the gentleman who can give me all this information? - Mr Archer."

Further on, Edwards continued;

> "What was it that led to that alteration in February 1907? Can you tell me? - I am sorry to say I cannot. This is rather an illustration of what I have said once or twice that I am anxious that questions of this kind should be put rather to the Officers who will follow me as experts on their particular points, than to me as an administrative officer."

(Brit Inq 22709- 22722)

Finally, delivering the coup de grace, Lord Mersey brought the questioning to a close;

> "I think we have had Sir Walter Howell nearly long enough."

(Brit Inq 22821-22)

Questioned over three days by the various legal counsel revealed less than anticipated with the notable exception that Sir Walter Howell, when it suited, did not know the answer himself but could refer the Court to someone who would know. It was not without a touch of irony that Sir Walter Howell was said to be a Fellow of the Royal Statistical Society, whose original seal, a wheatsheaf, with the motto *aliis exterendum*, which means "to be threshed out by others." Something it appears, Sir Walter Howell, in his position, practised dutifully.

(en.wikipedia.org/wiki/Walter_Jack_Howell)

Theatregoers at the Globe Theatre in London's West End at the time the Inquiry was taking place were enjoying the performance on stage of "*A Butterfly On The Wheel*," perhaps there were those in the Scottish Drill Hall during this episode who could have felt they were witnessing something similar, with the tormenting examination of Sir Walter Howell.

Despite his obvious lack of practical knowledge and obfuscation of the facts, nonetheless, his testimony before Lord Mersey was passed into the record. His career as an administrative bureaucrat in the highest offices of the Board of Trade continued; what remained of his credibility and reputation, however, was left much in doubt. A bachelor all his adult life, Sir Walter Howell died on January 29 the following year at the age of 59.

Yes Minister

"There are three kinds of falsehoods, lies, damned lies and statistics."

(Arthur James Balfour, 1st Earl of Balfour. Manchester Guardian, June 29, 1892.)

Following the disingenuous appearance of Sir Walter Howell on Day 26 of the British Inquiry, it was the turn of Sir Norman Hill, Chairman of the influential Merchant Shipping Advisory Committee. He was being asked by Mr Butler-Aspinall, co-counsel for the Board of Trade, if there were any figures published that showed the comparative loss of life at sea in emigrant ships and cargo ships.

(Brit Inq 24653)

Of course, counsel for the Board of Trade knew the answers beforehand. Like the Attorney-General and Sir Robert Finlay before him, he welcomed those figures being aired in public and entered into the official transcript.

There was no doubting the justification being put forth on behalf of the Board of Trade for the lack of lifeboats was the so-called "*immunity from lo*ss" of passenger-carrying vessels. Prompted by counsel, Sir Norman Hill was about to remind the Court why he believed it was so.

"Will you tell my Lord the reasons for that opinion of yours?"

"Well, My Lord, the best way of testing the practicability of it is, I think, to apply it to the existing ships afloat. Of course, one knows that with regard to cargo ships the boatage is based on life, and cargo ships have to carry enough boats on each side to accommodate all the lives on board."

The Commissioner said,

"If you based it on tonnage, you would provide a number of useless boats?"

"You would, a great many. On the other hand, if you are basing the boatage of the passenger ships, and still more of the emigrant ships, on the numbers carried, you should never have built the present class of passenger ship. May I take an example. The average size of the emigrant ship carrying 2,000 will be, say, 10,000 tons. Now if you are going to start from the numbers carried, 2,000, and you take 50 a boat, you have 40 boats. Now 40 boats on a 10,000-ton ship, 40 lifeboats, readily launchable boats, is an absolute impossibility; and you will find that still more so because it is not a difficulty only affecting the big emigrant ships; the same difficulty is affecting a substantial number of passenger ships. You will go down, My Lord, and you will find that they are boats of 3,000 tons carrying well over 1,000 people and carrying them very safely indeed."

Mr. Butler Aspinall;

"Then it comes to this, does it, Sir Norman, that it is practically impossible for an emigrant ship designed to carry 2,000 people, to carry lifeboats sufficient to hold those 2,000 people at one time? - With lifeboats readily available for launching, it is an absolute impossibility, I believe. Now, My Lord, if that is an unsafe ship, then you could prohibit her sailing the seas; but our view is, and of course, we had before us the records of these boats year after year, we have had in detail the 20 years' record, that we cannot say that that is an unsafe ship. If you compare the loss of life on that class of ship with a cargo-boat trading across the North Atlantic, with boat accommodation on each side for everybody on board, the loss of life in the emigrant ship, both amongst the crew and amongst the passengers, is a bagatelle compared with the loss of life on the other boat."

(Brit Inq 24650-2)

Sir Norman Hill's response speaks of the assuredness that stems from bureaucratic hubris and why there was an Inquiry into the loss of the *Titanic* in the first place. The newest and largest vessel afloat, shiny bright with the lingering whiff of fresh paint, lost at sea and only recently certified as 'seaworthy' by the same regulatory standards conceived by committees of 'experts' presided over by powerful men like Sir Norman Hill.

Counsel for the Board of Trade needed to impress on the mind of Lord Mersey of the "*bagatelle*" of shipping losses and score valuable points for their beleaguered client in the process. Lord Mersey appeared to be acquiescent to anything Sir Norman Hill had to say;

"I follow quite what you mean, he said. I do not know whether there are any statistics published - we have had some - to show the comparative loss of life at sea in emigrant ships and in cargo ships? Well,

My Lord, he began; I have worked them out very closely in detail. In the last 20 years, we find that there have been, as near as we can estimate, 32,000 voyages made by passenger ships across the Atlantic. That is 1,600 a year. There have been casualties either resulting in loss of life or resulting in the total loss of the ship without loss of life in 25 cases."
(Brit Inq 24653)
Sir Norman Hill made no offer of supportive evidence or declared his source for the figures he had stated, and tellingly he did not specify whether these losses were among British vessels alone. Without reference to the source of Sir Norman Hill's figures, some confusion exists in which class of vessel the figures are associated. Mr Butler-Aspinall enquired about comparing emigrant ships with cargo vessels. Sir Norman Hill replied with passenger ship numbers. Butler-Aspinall continued;

"Out of how many? - Out of 32,000 in 20 years. Twenty-five voyages have met with casualties resulting in either loss of life or total loss of the ship without loss of life."

Sir Norman reiterated, more for the benefit of the watchful Press corps than anyone else.

"Is that something less than one-tenth per cent? Butler-Aspinall speculated, "Yes, it is less than one in a thousand. Now, in those 25 casualties, the lives of 68 passengers and 80 of the crew were lost; that makes a total of 148."

The inclusion of crew members among the losses implies that passenger-carrying cargo vessels were counted in the figures.

The figures listed in the Board of Trade's documents (Table 1, page 263) reveal that, for the same period, from July 1891 to June 1911, there were 3 cases alone, in which more than 50 lives were lost, amounting to 192 officers and crew lost and 48 passengers. Sir Norman Hill gave his figures over a 20-year period where he claimed there were 25 casualties, in which 148 lives were lost. In the three incidents given by the Board of Trade alone, *Naronic*, *Mohegan* and *Huronian*, where 240 lives were lost, vastly exceeding the amount being put forward by Sir Norman Hill for the 25 casualties amounting to 148 lives lost over the same period. Where was he getting his information?

This testimony was suspiciously a smoke and mirrors exercise by Sir Norman Hill, conscious of the need to assuage the fears of the travelling public in the safety of passenger liners and to divert attention from failures in the ponderous workings of the various shipping Committees of which he was Chairman. Counsel continued;

"But if you include the "Titanic" your figures, of course, would be greater? - That is so, My Lord. In the same period, there were 233 casualties to other ships resulting in either loss of life or in total loss without loss of life, and in those casualties, there were 17 passengers and 1,275 crew lost, giving a total of 1,292."

A summary of Shipping Casualties (Departmental Paper No 250, p 303) provided by the Board of Trade for the 20 years ended June 30, 1911, amounts to 1,570 crew and 85 passengers. From what source the figures Sir Norman Hill was referring to when he dismisses the difference in numbers between emigrant vessels and passenger-carrying cargo vessels as a "*bagatelle*" is uncertain.

The Attorney-General spoke;

> "Will you give us the number of the ships as you did in the other case? - The total number of voyages?
> Yes? - No, I cannot; the total number of casualties is 233. Over what period? - Over 20 years."

(Brit Inq 24653-59)

The conceited tone in his reply to Lord Mersey's initial enquiry, "*Well, My Lord* he began, *I have worked them out very closely in detail,* " seems to fall flat on its face when he appears to struggle to break the figures down on request.

The Board of Trade Shipping Casualties (page 303) during the 20 years ended June 30, 1911, gives the number of casualties (involving total or partial loss of vessel) in which lives were lost as 258. This places serious doubt on the legitimacy of the 233 casualties and 1,292 lives lost coming from the Chairman of the Merchant Shipping Advisory Counsel compared to the 1,655 lives noted in the Board of Trade's table. Somewhere among the calculations, 25 vessels and 363 lives were excluded.

It stretches one's incredulity that the influential Chairman of a government-sponsored Committee of so-called 'experts' was working from shipping losses that were at best inaccurate or, at worse, duplicitous.

> "We cannot get the proportion? - No, I am doing my best to get it. It is a difficult figure to get at, but

I believe you will find that in the North Atlantic trade at least three-fourths of the voyages are in the passenger and the emigrant ships; they represent nearly three-fourths of the total. If it can be found anywhere, you will find it in the annual Navigation Returns. The figures that I have got from there are so striking - I mean it shows so few voyages from the other ships - that I am asking the Board to verify them for me."

Sir Norman Hill invited the Court to search the Navigation Returns to ascertain their totals. Unbelievably, he doubted the accuracy of his figures and was asking for verification from the Board of Trade, yet he was happy to quote them as factual to the Inquiry. We are again reminded of his confident opening remarks, "*I have worked them out very closely in detail.*"

A short period later, he was pleading, "*It is a difficult figure to get at.*"

There is an account of High Court Judge Baron Bramwell, of whom it is said, recognised three degrees in liars: "*the liar simple, the damned liar, and the expert witne*ss." Expert witnesses are called upon to give evidence based on their opinion and are therefore placed beyond accusations of perjury. Which, in the normal course of legal proceedings weighs heavily upon the ordinary witness, who can testify only to what they believe to be factual.

Any other interpretation of their evidence could attract charges of lying under oath.

Earlier, when he was giving evidence about the credentials of the members of the Advisory Committee, he was asked by Mr Scanlan;
> "You belong to the honourable profession of the Law, do not you? - I do, but since 1894 I have devoted a very great deal of my time to all matters affecting shipping, and I do really consider I am an expert on the statistics of shipping, but not on the building."

The Attorney-General: "I can vouch for that." The Commissioner added: "You are not likely to persuade me, Mr Scanlan, that Sir Norman Hill is not an expert on this matter. I know him to be an expert."
(Brit Inq 24766)

Curiously, someone who, in his own boastful words, is "*an expert on the statistics of shipping*" gave an unconvincing response regarding those same shipping figures when asked, under oath, in a Court of Inquiry. Instead of pressing him on his evidence, Sir Rufus Isaacs and Lord Mersey even endorsed him as an unimpeachable witness.

However, as Counsel on behalf of the National Sailors' and Firemen's Union of Great Britain and Ireland and Member of Parliament Thomas Scanlan was not likely to forget the rebuke from Lord Mersey. Later, when he was delivering his own summations during an exchange on the merits of Rule 12 pertaining to the provision of lifeboats. The Commissioner:
> "I can contemplate what Sir Norman Hill told us, that you may get the ship into such a condition of

congestion with lifeboats as to make it more dangerous than if there were no lifeboats at all."

Mr. Scanlan:

"I am very indisposed to take the view of Sir Norman Hill, who, for all that he has said about being an expert, is merely a lawyer."

The Commissioner: "What do you say? Merely a lawyer?"

Adroitly, Scanlan sidesteps a confrontation with Lord Mersey and explains;

"Insofar as the requisite knowledge to guide your Lordship in these matters is concerned, I ask your Lordship not to be, shall I say, led by lawyers in advising you as to what is practicable and safe to carry in the way of lifeboat accommodation. I would much rather impress upon your Lordship the view of Mr Wilding, or the view of Mr Sanderson, or the views of any of the other real experts we have had, especially the views of Mr Carlisle, than the view given by Sir Norman Hill. What does Sir Norman Hill know in comparison with Mr Wilding about the way in which the boat deck space on a ship like the "Titanic" could be utilised?"

(Final Arguments Day 36 p768)

At the commencement of his testimony, it was revealed that Sir Norman Hill was also secretary of the Liverpool Steamship Owners' Association and, since 1896, a member of the Shipowners' Parliamentary Committee. Two influential bodies represented the ship owner's interests in the corridors of power in Whitehall and the Houses of Parliament. The question of a conflict of interest never appeared to cause any concern. Any evidence that could be manipulated favourably to support the belief that Trans-Atlantic passage enjoyed "*immunity from loss*" was to be exploited.

Alex Issigonis* is said to have come up with the expression "*a camel is a horse designed by a committee,*" which might, not inappropriately, be confused with the various Committees tasked to provide "*expert advice*" to the Board of Trade decades previously. As he is also credited for stating; "*An expert is someone who tells you why you can't do something.*" The comparison becomes all the more applicable.

*(The designer of the BMC Mini car, first launched in 1959.)

Nonetheless, Lord Mersey remained unusually silent for this procrastination before him. We have read how he had berated others for similar, muddled presentations. Yet again, another witness, also titled, representing influential factions within Parliament and the Board of Trade, would enjoy unchallenged testimony that had a significant bearing on the absence of adequate lifeboats on passenger vessels in general and *Titanic* in particular.

Finally, Lord Mersey asked;

> "Can you speak generally as to the percentage of loss of life at sea as against the loss of life travelling on land? - No, My Lord, I never compared those. I can give you the loss of life at sea."

Lord Mersey added;

> "I do not suppose there are any reliable figures upon that subject." Clement Edwards said; "The figures are available for railways and mines on land, and also for sailors at sea."

"Yes, Lord Mersey said, but I am afraid they would be of very little use, because you could not find out what time the people on land had been travelling."
(Brit Inq 24656-66)

In his comment Clement Edwards was correct. The Board of Trade had records of rail accidents. From the years 1900 to 1911 there were 396 major accidents on the railways involving death and injuries where a Board of Trade investigation was carried out. Of the cases investigated by the Board of Trade there are 328 deaths recorded and 4,979 persons documented as having been injured.
(www.railwaysarchive.co.uk/eventsummary)

Before April 1912, munitions explosions and mining disasters contended with significant shipping losses for the greatest number of accidental deaths. When she slipped beneath the waves, the loss of the *Titanic* set the bar to a new level. This question had no bearing whatsoever on the Inquiry, and Lord Mersey would have interrupted and rebuked any other counsel for asking such a pointless question and wasting the Court's time. However, the information was available should anyone have been troubled to locate it. Adding some perspective to the discussion, James Thomas, Member of Parliament for Derby, mentioned railway men when he spoke in the Commons following the loss of the *Titanic*;

"This afternoon, every speaker was moved in asking for Board of Trade intervention because at a given moment, the nation was stirred by the awful disaster to the "Titanic". No hon. Member of this House would have pressed the Board of Trade in regard to the provision of life-saving appliances but for the fact that 1,400 people lost their lives at one moment. Does the House remember and realise that taking the last thirteen years, there has been no less than 6,286 railway men killed and 214,417 railway men injured in thirteen years. To put it in another way, every week there are nine railway men killed and 500 injured."

(Board Of Trade—Loss Of Life At Sea. HC Deb 21 May 1912 vol 38 cc1826)

A sobering rejoinder to the focus of attention being solely towards the losses from the *Titanic*.

During his testimony before Lord Mersey there were no formal submissions as to the source of Sir Norman Hill's findings, and incredibly, as was revealed, even he was uncertain of their accuracy. Whatever misrepresentations Sir Norman Hill was passing-off to the Inquiry were accepted as factual without the need for further elaboration by Lord Mersey and members of the Court; we can, therefore, justifiably question their validity. We have only the supposed submission of documents by Sir Walter Howell and the figures he quoted as a template that broadly corresponds to those documents stored in the National Archives. Three separate witnesses, three different sets of figures, each was proposing the low incidence of casualty at sea as vindication for the stagnation of legislation to keep pace with increases in ship's scale and passenger numbers.

In regard to the shipping figures, the tallest tree in the forest is only the tallest tree in that forest, not necessarily all forests. The figures given by Sir Norman Hill et al., were not categorical or beyond challenge.

Many of these policies and practices followed a vessel out to sea, and ships' masters had almost free reign to interpret much of their meaning. For Captain Smith, the passengers and crew aboard the *Titanic*, his "*mistake*" ended abruptly only days into their voyage with calamitous results.

Barely two weeks had passed since news of the loss of the *Titanic* had broken when Sir Arthur Fell, Conservative MP for Great Yarmouth, asked the question in Parliament;

> "How many passengers crossed the Atlantic between the United Kingdom and the United States and Canada in the ten years ending December 31, 1911, and the number of lives lost among such passengers except from natural causes; and what percentage such loss bears to the number of passengers?"

In his reply, Mr Buxton said:

> "The total number of passengers of all classes and all nationalities carried outward and inward on board British and foreign ships between the United Kingdom and the United States and Canada (including Newfoundland) during the ten years ending December 31, 1911, was 6,053,382, of which the great proportion were carried in United Kingdom, ships. The number of passengers reported to the Board of Trade as having lost their lives by casualties to vessels belonging to the United Kingdom (I cannot give those on other ships) on voyage between the United Kingdom and the United States and Canada during the period named was nine."

(Passenger Losses (Atlantic). April 29, 1912. Loss of the steamship "Titanic")
The information shared by the President of the Board of Trade in his reply is strikingly similar to figures stated by officials called before Lord Mersey's Inquiry which would convene days later at the beginning of May.
(MT9/920F Table 2 Page 264)
The compilation of which has been previously exhausted in this chapter. The numbers quoted in Parliament would also go unchallenged or further elaboration. What is interesting to note is that Sydney Buxton, like those who would follow giving testimony in Lord Mersey's Court, would mangle any useful meaning from the figures by the casual use of terms such as; "British and foreign ships" then only include numbers from "United Kingdom ships." Or "passenger vessels" and "emigrant vessels," the definition of which was routinely misplaced.

Like many politicians, Sydney Buxton also evaded the original question, "*how many passengers and the number of lives that were lost among such passengers.*" In his response, he had whittled down the 6,053,382 total number of passengers to only those "*vessels belonging to the United Kingdom*" claiming "*I cannot give those on other ships.*" We can be reasonably certain there were not two different scales of shipping losses produced, one for Sydney Buxton and another for the Inquiry.

We know the latter part of the 19th century saw the beginnings of long-overdue improvements in ship safety. From 1850, the Admiralty had been responsible for compiling records of shipping losses, a duty which devolved to the Board of Trade through the Merchant

Shipping Act of 1854. For the first time, registers, and summary abstracts (Board of Trade Casualty Returns) provided a centralised record to glean a statistical overview of shipwrecks and identify common trends in shipping casualties. Regular or frequent losses, and measures to reduce hazards to shipping adopted, such as building lighthouses, placing marker buoys etc. From that, you would be forgiven for thinking there would be some mutually comparative data between the Board of Trade and Lloyd's Register; it seems not so.

Similarly, a further amendment of the Merchant Shipping Act of 1876 enforced the compulsory marking of a load line on British ships to remove the practice of putting out to sea overloaded 'coffin ships,' or unseaworthy vessels that all too often foundered with all hands. The load line, which is still in use, albeit in a refined form today, is better known as the 'Plimsoll Line' after the M.P. Samuel Plimsoll, who had campaigned for many years to achieve its adoption.

Therefore, other than their own Wreck Reports, the Board of Trade had access to several resources from which they could assemble the information they sought. For example, Lloyd's Register's Casualty Returns were updated quarterly, and records would show reported losses.

The Board of Trade held responsibility for the general superintendence of matters relating to merchant ships and seamen. This included overseeing formal investigations into any shipping casualties on or near the coasts of the United Kingdom and for any British ship stranded, damaged, or lost.

To understand where Sir Norman Hill was placed in the hierarchy of responsibility and how we look at his evidence before Lord Mersey's Inquiry, we must look at his fuller statement before Lord Mersey, Examined by Mr Butler Aspinall.

> "Are you the Chairman of the Merchant Shipping Advisory Committee? - Yes. Has your Committee been amassing and collecting together information about life-saving appliances and matters connected with making navigation safe at sea? - Yes. The Committee only deals with the matters upon which the board asks for its opinion. It has since 1907, consulted us on a number of points. At the present moment, it has asked us to advise generally upon the Life-Saving Rules and also generally as to whether we can make any suggestions to increase the precautions that are taken to protect life at sea. It has only asked us since the loss of the "Titanic" to advise generally. Before that had you collected a great deal of evidence and information?" - Oh yes, we have advised on many points connected with boats and manning, and such things."

(Brit Inq 24564)

Why then was it so difficult for someone in the position that Sir Norman Hill had occupied for so many years to obtain accurate, concise information for presentation to the Court? Unless, of course, he had and chose not to share the data he acquired. Sir Norman Hill was an inveterate bureaucrat who stamped his presence on the workings of the Merchant Shipping Advisory Committee over many years. Crucial years in the development of large passenger vessels, the likes of which had never been seen before or had legislation in place to keep pace with their enormous growth. Afterall, he had access to a "*great deal of evidence*" by his own admission.

Regarding his figures, he said, with a hint of pomposity, "*I have worked them out very closely in detail.*" When asked for clarification on another point, he replied, "*I am doing my best to get it. It is a difficult figure to get at.*" What beggars' belief is that Lord Mersey did not intervene and insist on clarity from the witness. When Sir Walter Howell was on the stand, he felt the combined wrath of his interrogators when he dilly-dallied with his responses.

The conclusion that the Court afforded Sir Norman Hill extraordinary latitude due to his position and influence cannot be overlooked and that another possibility exists. The Board of Trade knew when the *Titanic* sank that they would come under intense scrutiny. No more so than for the dilatory monitoring of these changes in vessel proportions and the need for regulations that kept abreast of these changes. The possibility exists somewhere in Whitehall, more precisely, the Marine Department of the Board of Trade. Sir Walter Howell and, to a lesser extent, Sir Norman Hill, who, as Chairman of the Advisory Committee, could remain concealed behind the *in-camera* exclusivity of the Committee's deliberations, were able to falsely represent the figures of shipping losses to mutually minimise its impact on their careers. That they were successful is a shameful indictment of the entire Inquiry process, and, if, as this author believes, is true, the complicity in an official 'cover-up ' at their level is plain to see. A trail of clues leading to conspiracy and obfuscation from the higher offices of H.M. Government in Whitehall to the shifting decks of the sinking *Titanic*.

Sir Norman Hill's career survived this debacle. His presence among the British delegation representing Britain's interests in the first international Safety of Life At Sea (SOLAS) conference in 1913-14 is evidence of that. His name appears in the documentation alongside another stalwart from the British Inquiry, Lord Mersey himself.
(www.ukwhoswho.com)

And Finally?

"Falsehood flies and truth comes limping after it."

(Jonathan Swift.)

When the last witness called before the Inquiry finished their testimony, the floor, as it were, was opened for the various counsel to summarise their conclusions to Lord Mersey before he retired to consider his verdict. Conceivably this was the last opportunity for those representatives to remind the Wreck Commissioner of testimony conducive to their preferences as to the outcome.

During his summations on Day 36 of the evidence presented before the Inquiry, the Attorney-General appeared to be defensive of the decisions made by the Board of Trade before the events of April 1912. The message was that the shipping figures spoke the truth about the safety of life at sea and the vindication of the Board of Trade's decisions over many years.

The Attorney-General:

"The precautions that the Board of Trade were providing under their Regulations, and that the scale which was in force under their Regulations were sufficient because your Lordship will have appreciated this - take, for example, the last ten years from 1902 to 1911 - that during those ten years there had been over 6,000,000 passengers carried, and a large number of them, of course, carried in larger vessels than had existed at any rate before 1904."

Presumably, Sir Rufus Isaacs was basing his assertions on those same shipping figures perpetuated by the Board of Trade and tenuously referred to by Sir Walter Howell. That being so, the Attorney-General failed in his remit firstly to substantiate the evidence presented and, where any malfeasance is exposed, actively pursue avenues of investigation which exposed those officials responsible.

It appears no one, from reading the official inquiry transcripts, sought to question the accuracy of those statistics placed before Lord Mersey. Those members of Parliament who asked whether the British Inquiry could be impartial in its deliberations of the allegations of ineptitude and deception against its most senior Board of Trade bureaucrats had much to contemplate as the Inquiry unfolded.

Only once was there any exploration of the content; it came from Lord Mersey himself when he asked the Attorney-General, during his summation, why he was confining his observations to the Atlantic trade only. Making the point that global maritime trade would involve a much larger number of vessels to which the same Board of Trade rules applied, these regulations were not exclusive to the Atlantic trade.

The Commissioner: "When you say carried, are you confining your observations to the Atlantic trade?

The Attorney-General: Yes.

The Commissioner: I thought so, because there must have been an enormous number, a much larger number, carried over the surface of the globe.

The Attorney-General: Yes.

The Commissioner: To which these Rules apply.

The Attorney-General: I quite appreciate that.

The Commissioner: These Rules are not confined to the Atlantic?

The Attorney-General: "No, but we have only the figures of the North Atlantic. The only figures we have are for the voyages on this route; that is why I am referring to them. They are very, very significant I submit."

The Attorney-General's response to Lord Mersey's prescient observation was to duplicitously admit, rather unconvincingly, that they only have the figures for the North Atlantic available and "*they are very, very significant.*"

He then continued, disregarding the very legitimate point the Commissioner had made. At times, throughout the Inquiry, Lord Mersey had displayed his customary annoyance at counsel for straying off the point or not asking witnesses relevant questions, particularly, but not exclusively, to those who represented the seamen's unions and roundly rebuked them. Here, the Commissioner had speculated about global merchant marine casualties even commenting, "*there must have been an enormous number.*" In a novel role reversal, the Attorney-General dismissed his query, admonishing him by saying, "*they are very, very significant.*" Not for the first time, decisions which would attract accusations that it had been the Attorney-General who set the Inquiries agenda and led the Wreck Commissioner through the proceedings towards its sterile conclusions were evident.

Accusations of official concealment of Board of Trade incompetence were to follow the publication of the findings of the British Inquiry. No better evidence exists of such an occurrence than the interpretation and manipulation of the shipping statistics. Regardless of this blatant fallacy, the Attorney-General pressed on;

"During those 10 years, of the 6,000,000 passengers carried, he said, more than half of them were carried in vessels that belonged to the United Kingdom."

Whether Sir Rufus Isaacs was deliberately only referring to vessels owned and operated by British shipping lines and excluding vessels that had been built by British firms although operated by foreign-owned shipping lines was unclear. Technically, the White Star Line did not "*belong to the United Kingdom*" and had been part of the I.M.M corporation since 1902. Sanderson claimed during his testimony that 2,179,594 passengers had been carried by White Star vessels in the period 1901-1911.

The Commissioner had asked the question as to whether it was possible to separate the number of passengers into those carried in British vessels and those carried in other ships, and the Attorney-General explained;

"That the figures are not available for doing that, and he added; we have not been able to get them, and the result is we have to take it in this way, that over 6,000,000 passengers were carried during those ten years, that is the last ten years, and that more than half of them, and considerably more than half, were carried in British vessels."

When giving evidence, Harold Sanderson had no difficulty presenting voyages and passenger numbers on behalf of the White Star Line. Could the same not have been done for the other major shipping lines? Considering the amount of time and effort spent trying to establish the identity of the 'mystery vessel', purported to have been seen by *Titanic* survivors. Foreign governments were contacted, and shipping lines were asked about the whereabouts of their vessels at the time of the sinking. Every avenue, it appeared, was explored in a futile and patently time-wasting exercise in distraction. The same enthusiasm to find answers about shipping losses would have reaped much more relevant information for the Inquiry to ponder. However, the answers were already known if anyone cared to look among Lloyd's and the Board of Trade's records of the history of sea passages over many years. No one, it appears, wanted to dig too deeply to uncover the truth. The Attorney-General, based on this information, was feeding Lord Mersey and the Inquiry a diet of evidence from a menu of his choosing.

It appeared this was the only information the Attorney-General wanted to present to the Court and have entered into the record. His following statement makes that clear. "*We do know the number of lives lost in British vessels, and that is nine during those ten years. That is the point I wanted to bring to your Lordship's attention.*" (Authors Italics)

Had the Commissioner been more exacting and insisted on scrutiny of the information on shipping casualties to non-British vessels on the North Atlantic route and across the world, one example, he would have discovered that among those losses was the *Norge*, mentioned previously. Had those casualties been included in the totals given by the Attorney-General, the loss of over 620 lives would surely have made a sad and telling impression upon the Court.
(Dictionary of Disasters at Sea During the Age of Steam: 1824-1962, Vol 1I M-Z. Charles Hocking, 1969)

The Attorney-General went on to explain the view that they (the Board of Trade) took;

"Was that it was much more important that they should have vessels constructed with efficient watertight compartments than have a larger provision of boats."

Again, he reminded the Court that the view that Sir Alfred Chalmers took was that it;

"Was not possible to have a larger number of boats without interfering with the vessel, without hampering her decks, and without, at any rate, providing boats which he thought it would be very difficult to launch. The result is this, he said; that very few lives were lost, and the importance of it is, that fewer lives were lost during those ten years than in the preceding ten years."

That the views of both the Board of Trade and the shipowners were in agreement should come as no surprise as Sir Alfred Chalmers had been the major exponent of a 'bulkheads before boats' policy and had promulgated his rationale of the relative safety of trans-Atlantic passage as justification for pursuing the token 'fig-leaf' numbers of lifeboats on passenger vessels. Harold Sanderson had conceded that lifeboats would not support the number of passengers they were rated for in the first place. The policy of not supplying sufficient boats as in the past would win the day, and no less than the Attorney-General was the standard-bearer. The Commissioner had also apparently 'drank the Kool-Aid' and swallowed the Attorney-General's shameful proposition.

We can surmise this as it was Lord Mersey himself who reminded the Court that Sir Robert Finlay had used those figures to show how "*negatively good*" the system of steaming ahead without taking into account the possibility of there being ice on the track, expecting to see it well enough in advance to take avoiding action. We know how that turned out.

A reply to a letter of April 25, only days after the *Titanic* went down, from Sir Walter Howell to the Merchant Shipping Advisory Service sent in response to an inquiry regarding a revision of the boat scales states;

> "The Committee fully recognise that the proved impossibility of keeping such a vessel as the "Titanic" afloat, after a collision with ice, until the arrival of outside succour, has created an entirely new situation which was neither in the contemplation of the Board of Trade nor of the Committee in the consideration of the extension of the existing boat scale in regard to vessels of 10,000 tons and upwards."

(Sir Walter Howell April 27, 1912. MT9/920F)

An admission that the prospect of a large vessel coming to grief following a collision with an iceberg in the North Atlantic had "*created an entirely new situation*" which was "*neither in the contemplation of the Board of Trade nor of the Committee*" defies belief in its staggering naivety and obtuseness.

What is difficult to comprehend is the fixation that endured with collisions at sea with ice which White Star counsel suggested falsely that it was a rare event. However, it occurred, in the North Atlantic at least, only during certain months of the year, while shipping continued all year-round and was exposed to all sorts of other climatic and physical hazards. Finlay was protecting the White Star Line from accusations of negligent navigation because the *Titanic* struck an iceberg when too far north and going excessively fast for the reported conditions; the presence of which they had been warned about at that time of year in the location that ice should have been anticipated. What was there to defend?

Finally, it was the Attorney-General who reminded the Court that;

"*These arguments stand very well until you get a disaster of this character.*" Then, he went on to say, "*no doubt, you have got totally different considerations to apply,*" and the only use I am intending to make of it is not to say it is unnecessary to provide for their boat accommodation in the future, but I am putting it before you for your Lordship's consideration, as, at least, evidence which justified the Board of Trade, if it had been right in its opinion upon the material which it hitherto had had, in coming to the conclusion that further boat accommodation was not necessary in vessels of 10,000 tons. That is all I want to say about it," he concluded.

However, that tortuous assertion was only relevant if the "*evidence which justified the Board of Trade*" was an accurate representation of the facts, not a contrived excuse for failures to update regulations, or in Sir Robert Finlay's case, for negligent navigation, in areas known to be populated with ice.

Mr Butler-Aspinall, counsel for the Board of Trade, when soliciting the answers from Sir Norman Hill. Answers, it could be construed, served the Board of Trade's pleadings for the innocence of wrongdoing. There is little doubt that the figures "*difficult to get at* " were adjusted with the prevarication on display. It was not the only time. We have only the explanation given by the Attorney-General to trust that the figures were really "*not available*" for a more precise breakdown. And how he was able to state with such confidence; that "*more than half of them, considerably more half of them*" were carried in British ships.

Contemporary records from the National Archives reveal that the figures quoted in Court were inaccurate or incomplete. The real question was whether the Inquiry was denied access or chose to ignore them.

This part of the Inquiry was weighted heavily in favour of the Board of Trade and is not difficult to see. None more so than in the presentation of the shipping figures. When we look closely at the evidence given by Sir Norman Hill, even if we accept the premise of almost 32,000 relatively safe crossings, a vessel needs only to get into difficulty on one occasion for its passengers and crew to be placed in serious jeopardy. The risk was an inherent part of ocean passage and one that was understood but not welcomed by most travellers. The genuine concern should have been whether these were excessive losses due to preventable causes, such as those under investigation. As the saying goes, even a stopped clock shows the correct time twice a day!

In the years 1902-1911, according to Lloyd's Register, in British vessels alone, there were 1432 shipping casualties from various causes, including collision, foundered, lost, missing, and wrecked.

(Lloyd's Register of British and Foreign Shipping. Returns Of Vessels Totally Lost, Condemned, &C. 1902-1911)

Of course, not all casualties would have resulted in the loss of life. Lloyd's Register, as comprehensive as it is, does not routinely record lives lost. However, in those same years, those identical records show there were 163 ships reported as lost or missing, which we remind ourselves, presumes that all on board, passengers, and crew, are also victims. Board of Trade figures* list ten vessels as missing during that same 10-year interval, with the loss of 199 crew and two passengers. Where Sir Norman's 25 casualties and 148 deaths, over 20 years, originates is unknown. For the same 20-year period, involving the exact nature of loss, Lloyd's records 3,166 incidents involving British vessels alone. Worldwide the number leaps to 13,083 or 9,917 if we exclude the British figures.

*(Shipping Casualties pages 330-1)

Those "*Statistics compiled in connection with the S.S. Titanic Inquiry showing loss of life in the British Trans-Atlantic passenger trade;* Departmental Paper No 250 page 303 gives a total for all vessels, registered in the U.K., both sail and steam, during the 20 years ended June 30, 1911, on voyages between European ports to the US, Canada, and Newfoundland to be 432 vessels; where 258 of these casualties' involved loss of life, totalling 1,570 officers and crew and 85 passengers. Why Sir Norman Hill would disregard the Board of Trade figures and present to the Court another set of numbers that were never questioned or elaborated upon. Remember, Sir Norman Hill's testimony came after Sir Walter Howell, whom we know, during his testimony, alluded to those same figures. We also know the Attorney-General was present during both witnesses' giving evidence. Even he did not see fit to query the numbers, the silence deafening.

The "*other ships*" he mentions, we assume to be non-British registered vessels. If the "*same period*" includes the twenty years before he *Titanic*, there are several notable examples of great loss of life among foreign vessels. In the following cases alone, the figures presented do not add up. The German passenger vessel *Elbe*, another 'Clydebuilt' ship, by John Elder & Co, on route from Bremerhaven via Southampton to New York, collided with the steamship *Crathie* in foul weather on January 13, 1895. The *Elbe* sunk within 20 minutes of the collision, and only 20 who had made it to the one remaining lifeboat survived. In total, 332 perished.

Another notable foreign-going passenger calamity of the same twenty-year period includes; the French vessel, *La Bourgogne* sailing from New York to Le Harve, which sank with 549 victims following a collision in the early hours of the morning of July 4, 1898, in dense fog. Include the *Norge* with the loss of 620 lives, and between those three tragic events alone, the *Elbe*, *La Bourgogne* and *Norge*, spanning ten years, up to 1905, 1501 lives were lost. Indeed, a "Titanic" scale of events. That was, of course, all before the *Titanic* sank, taking the lives of 1490 souls to the watery deep at one stroke, and the ripples created by her demise reached all the way to Whitehall, lapping around the blameworthy feet of officials such as Sir Walter Howell et al.

Any lingering doubts that only the lives of passengers travelling 'cabin class' counted was justified when one newspaper cried;

FIVE LOST FROM CUNARD LINER GREAT SEAS SWEEP OVER OCEAN STEAMER

"Five lives are known to have been lost and more than thirty persons Injured, one fatally and some of them seriously, on the Cunard line steamer Campania last Wednesday, when a gigantic wave rolled over the steamer and swept across a deck thick with steerage passengers. So sudden was the coming of the disaster and so great the confusion which attended and followed it that even the officers of the steamer themselves were unable today upon the vessel's arrival here to estimate the full extent of the tragedy. It is possible that the five persons known to be missing from the steerage may not constitute the full number of dead. When the Campania reached quarantine today ten of the injured passengers were still in the ship hospital, some of them seriously hurt and a score of others were nursing minor Injuries."

The article continued;

"Wednesday's disaster marks the first time in the Cunard line's history of more than sixty years that a passenger has been lost from one of its steamers by accident.
Although some of the passengers thought that the Campania should have stopped in an attempt to save those who were washed overboard, the officers say that this was practically an Impossibility. Both passengers and officers say that the waves in Wednesday afternoon's gale were the highest they had ever seen. At times they broke as high as the top of the smokestacks. An hour before the accident a second officer on the bridge was struck by the descending crest of a wave, knocked down and rendered unconscious. Many steerage passengers upon landing today fell upon their knees and offered prayers of thanksgiving over their safe arrival."

(Los Angeles Herald, October 15, 1905, recovered from cdnc.ucr.edu)

The number of those lost remained vague and names went unrecorded.

The drama continued. "28 in the Campania's Steerage Hurt, 10 of Them Seriously."

(Great Sea Sweeps Liner. New York Times, October 14, 1905)

"On Wednesday October 11, 1905, on a voyage from Liverpool to New York a large wave washed 7 people overboard and several other passengers was serious injured. The ship arrived in New York on Friday morning."

(norwayheritage.com)

On February 4, 1905, the 1179grt Furness Withy passenger vessel *Damara* foundered off Sable Island, while on a voyage from London to Halifax, struck Musquodoboit Ledge, 5 miles off Jeddore in a snowstorm and sank. Fifteen (including the Captain) died in a lifeboat that never made it to land. 19 crew members survived but were found to be frostbitten.

There were, we know, other casualties in those preceding two decades, mercifully, not as significant a loss in human terms, extreme as these three examples were. However, it makes a mockery of the statistics provided by Sir Norman Hill and, incredibly, accepted as a true account by the Court. It was not purely British xenophobia that precluded foreign vessels from the calculations, as during the Inquiry, for example, enquiries were made on how foreign shipbuilders viewed watertight bulkheads. One can conclude it had to be purely to minimise the actual numbers of losses of passenger vessels from all nations, including German, Danish and French.

A conservative figure of 2,694 for all lives lost on passenger vessels alone plying the North Atlantic between 1890 and 1910. A figure vastly greater than those presented by both Sir Norman Hill and J. Walter Howell. Add the 1,490 souls believed lost when the *Titanic* foundered, and the number rises dramatically to 4,184. It is worth repeating that it is reasonable to include shipping lines flying flags other than British as the hazards are the same and vessels registered other than in the U.K. have similar regulations for seaworthiness. As we have read, most were constructed in British yards, so it is not worth splitting hairs over such an important detail.

Many of these vessel's losses made headline news at the time, raising safety concerns among the travelling public and alarm to the shipping industry, mindful of anything that might affect passenger numbers. There was shamefully little comment on these figures in the Scottish Drill Hall. Not even those representing seamen; Scanlan, Lewis and Clement Edwards usually alert for slippery deeds from the Board of Trade.

If this were the case, it is possible that specific legislation known to the Marine Department was delayed or shelved and this was not exclusively down to Sir Walter Howell. We know Sir Alfred Chalmers had strong views on what he felt was right for maritime policy. The powerful shipping lobby in Parliament appeared to have been satisfied because there were no successful moves during his time in office to have regulations introduced or updated.

Why the Board of Trade would promulgate falsehood is not difficult to understand. However, the deception continued throughout the Inquiry. It is difficult to imagine the Attorney-General missing such flagrant discrepancies from professional members of the Board of Trade unless he understood the reasoning behind it and went along with the charade for expedience.

Those figures quoted by the members of the Board of Trade were suitably disguised in various forms. Namely, by excluding those passengers not travelling as first-class, but not crew members or officers, only counting losses exceeding 50 lives or only looking at selected vessels and excluding voyages on other routes and destinations.

All ships plying their trade across the North Atlantic recognised as one of the world's most treacherous stretches of ocean, faced the same perils. Some of these ships were better equipped to survive the hazards, and some were newer and featured more modern design features. Many more were skilfully navigated, and the rest were just plain lucky.

It seemed the Board of Trade was under attack from all sides, the paradox of being accused of not doing enough by the public, press and seafarers' trades unions and threatening to do too much by the shipowner's representatives.

During the Parliamentary debate into Lord Mersey's Report Canadian-born M.P for Gravesend Sir Gilbert Parker commented;

> "If one reads the letters written by the Board of Trade to the Advisory Committee previous to the disaster, we recognise the fact that Sir Alfred Chalmer's views, as placed before Lord Mersey were the views that were held by everybody connected with the Board of Trade and with the Advisory Committee. Lord Mersey refers with great care to Sir Alfred Chalmers, and says, in effect, that he can understand the point of view. The point of view is

this:- "We think that it was not the right or the duty of the State to impose regulations so long as the record of the shipping company was a clean one— in other words that there were few accidents. Really, we who come to look at the thing now from the standpoint of after results must feel a sense of humiliation that our experts should have relied upon immunity from accidents."
(Lord Mersey's Report. HC Deb 07 October 1912 vol 42 col 78)

Of the many speakers who would present their views during the Debate, few would have the acceptance from both sides of the House for the collective wisdom of his words which transcended party politics.

There could be no defence that shipowners could produce that would discredit the economy of words and simplicity of reason, which Sir Gilbert Parker used to condense the arguments down to the very essence of what the public, the Government and the shipowners should be prepared to accept for the future safety of sea voyages.

That "*our experts should have relied upon immunity from accidents*" was pertinently absent from any of Lord Mersey's deliberations or by other speakers months later in the House during the Debate into the Report.

Alexander Wilkie, former ships carpenter and now Member of Parliament for Dundee,* one of the first-ever Labour MP's elected in Scotland and held this seat for 16 years said;

"Just to show the position taken up when a question was asked at the "Titanic" Inquiry of Sir Alfred Chalmers whether the "Titanic " disaster led him to believe that any single one of the Board's regulations should be modified, he distinctly answered "No."

The next question was: "Are there no lessons to be learned from this disaster?" – "No, because it is an extraordinary one." The Marine Department of the Board of Trade, we were told, guarded against ordinary occurrences and not extraordinary occurrences. Striking an iceberg is not an extraordinary occurrence. It has often occurred in the history of the mercantile marine, and therefore it ought to have been within the purview of the officials of the Marine Department, who ought to have provided for such an occasion. That shows the attitude that has been adopted, and that apparently has satisfied the shipowners."

(Lord Mersey's Report. HC Deb 07 October 1912 vol 42 col 124)
*(From 1908 to 1922, his colleague as MP for Dundee was former President of the Board of Trade and future British Prime Minster, Winston Churchill. Then a Liberal M.P.)

Mr Frederick Jowett (Labour M.P. Bradford West) commented;

"The last question I remember was put by the hon. Member for Devizes. (Basil Peto) His question led the President of the Board of Trade to state that there had been actually less loss of life since the change was made than before. When that statement is examined carefully it will be seen that the instances referred to by the President of the Board were confined to those washed overboard. If he had carried his investigation further and answered the question put, he would have had to confess that there had been a distinct increase in the loss of life taking all classes of life lost together."

(Lord Mersey's Report. HC Deb 07 October 1912 vol 42 col 148)
M.P. Leslie Scott, a ship owner and opponent of Sydney Buxton's draft recommendations and the implementation of new legislation said during the debate in Parliament;
"The great increase in safety at sea shown by the records is due, I believe, entirely to the increase in the safety of ships themselves and has nothing whatever to do with boats and life-saving accommodation. Since 1890, although the boat accommodation has been increased, the number of lives saved by the boats has decreased. Secondly, there is no evidence, up to the case of the "Titanic", of any life having, since 1890, been lost by an insufficient number of boats. Thirdly, out of 9,000,000 passengers carried during the last twenty years—this number of passengers may possibly include the crews—only 118 lives have been lost up to the time of the "Titanic". These lives were lost in three casualties, with the exception of single individuals who were washed overboard. That is the record of the last twenty years. It is, therefore, madness to endanger the security of the ship for the sake of doing what is suggested, even if you succeeded in increasing the chances of safety and getting away from the ship when she went down."
(Lord Mersey's Report. HC Deb 07 October 1912 vol 42 col 46)

Leslie Scot gave a figure of 118 lives lost over twenty years, which occurred in 3 incidents. Which three incidents we can only speculate. Presumably, these were vessels on the North Atlantic routes. The closest comparison would be the *Naronic*, *Mohegan* and *Huronian*, where, as we have seen previously, 240 passengers and crew were lost. As the saying goes, never let the facts get in the way of a good story.

Either way, Sydney Buxton unceremoniously shut down Scott's argument in his reply;

> "The hon. Member for Liverpool quoted figures showing how very safe it was to travel by sea. We all rejoice that that should be so. The hon. Member pointed out that in the last twenty years only 118 passengers and crew had lost their lives in crossing the Atlantic. That is a very fine record. But unfortunately, we cannot now use that argument at all, because in one year the number has gone up from 118 for twenty years, to 1,500 in one, and we must take warning by such a calamity."

(Lord Mersey's Report. HC Deb October 7, 1912, Vol 42 Cc32-148)

The nine million passengers conveyed in 1890-1912 broadly agrees with those figures (Table 2, page 264) inferred by Sir Walter Howell during his testimony before Lord Mersey. However, the 118 casualties in the three cases do not add up. Sir Walter Howell quoted a figure of 82 lives lost in those twenty years for British vessels plying their trade on the North Atlantic route, and for the same period for all ships, 240 lives were lost. Sir Norman Hill quoted a figure of 148 lives for that same period among British vessels involving 25 casualties; not all resulted in the loss of life.

During the same October debate and demonstrating the skills of diplomatic subterfuge and blunt pragmatism that would come to the fore when he would later be instrumental in the dissemination of propaganda as a means which helped to bring the United States into the First World War Sir Gilbert Parker said;

"This afternoon, when I listened to the hon. Member for Hexham (Holt), upon my word I felt appalled, and for this reason. The Member for Hexham—and he said the same last spring—said in effect, "What is the good of all your rules? What is the good of all your appliances? For the last twenty years there has been so small a loss of life." He described the appliances as rubbish. Had he forgotten the "Oceana" in the English Channel, where, through lack of organisation, human lives were lost? But the lives that were saved were saved by the rules of the Board of Trade, which required that boats be carried, and the hon. Member talked about the "Titanic," and said that lives would not have been saved had there been a rough sea. Is that any reason why boats should not be supplied for those who were saved?"

(Lord Mersey's Report. HC Deb 07 October 1912 vol 42 col 76)

The S.S. *Oceana* was a P&O passenger liner and cargo vessel, built in 1888 by Harland and Wolff of Belfast. Originally assigned to carry passengers and mail between London and Australia, she was later assigned to routes between London and British India.

On 16 March 1912, the ship collided in the Strait of Dover with the *Pisagua*, a 2,850 grt German-registered four-masted

steel-hulled barque. As a result, *Oceana* sank off Beachy Head on the East Sussex coast, with the loss of nine lives.
(Wrecksite – Oceana Ocean Liner 1888-1912)

During his final summation, Sir Robert Finlay took the opportunity to mention the shipping figures;

> "I say with some confidence that no one can take these three sets of statistics with regard to the absence of casualties, the very small number of deaths on passages across the Atlantic relatively to the enormous traffic when this system was being uniformly pursued of going right ahead in clear weather at the same speed – no one, I say, can look at those statistics and fail to see that they were perfectly justified, these men of experience in this particular branch of navigation, the North Atlantic, in their belief that in clear weather you could see the ice in time to avoid it. If that were not the case, you could not have had such statistics as those which are before the Court."

He continued;

> "The experience in this matter is worth any amount of theory about it. Here you have this uniform practice of 20 years, and you have, I venture to say, an extraordinary absence of casualty. It is perfectly impossible that you could have had that low percentage of casualties if the system on which they were proceeding was not a sound one. And it was sound, because in clear weather you could see a berg in time to avoid it. That is my submission to your Lordship on that part of the case."

Sir Robert Finlay would round it all up and plead before Lord Mersey on Day 30 of the Inquiry, that the "*uniform practice*" which most Trans-Atlantic ships masters followed meant that Captain Smith could not be guilty of negligence; "*doing that which had been done by every vessel in this trade for a long series of years.*" Stating; "*to the fact that it had worked well and given admirable results in practice.*" The "*practice*" he alluded to was driving your vessel at full speed and only reducing speed when visibility becomes reduced. In defence of his proposition, he trotted out statistics in Court of the safe passage that "*worked well,*" "with so-called "*admirable results,*" achieved by the vast majority of shipping lines avoiding catastrophe regularly for many years.

Using evidence from the testimony of Sir Walter Howell, the White Star counsel told the Court that the statistics (produced by the Board of Trade) showed that from 1892 to 1901 three and a quarter million passengers were carried across the Atlantic. During that time, he quoted, only 73 (lives) were lost.

> "Ice, Sir Robert Finlay said, is more frequent between April to August, less than half of the year and shipping lanes are adjusted further south to avoid the most likely locations of drifting ice."

In October, during the scheduled Parliamentary debate into Lord Mersey's Report, M.P. Leslie Scott also quoted some interesting statistics, again unsupported with documentary evidence;

> "Twenty years ago, the average annual loss of life in the British mercantile marine was 2,000. Today it is 700. The number of casualties involving loss of life

twenty years ago, year by year, was on average 321. Today it is 145, or less than half. And those figures can only be appreciated if at the same time we bear in mind that the number of voyages performed per annum by British ships has enormously increased and that today the average is well over a quarter of a million."

He continued;

"Since 1890, although the boat accommodation has been increased, he said, the number of lives saved by the boats has decreased. Secondly, there is no evidence, up to the case of the "Titanic" of any life having, since 1890, been lost by an insufficient number of boats. Thirdly, out of 9,000,000 passengers carried during the last twenty years—this number of passengers may possibly include the crews—only 118 lives have been lost up to the time of the "Titanic."

(Lord Mersey's Report. HC Deb October 07, 1912, vol 42 cc34)

The 9,000,000 passengers could have come from the Board of Trade's figures, which records between 1892 and 1911, 6,178,004 westbound and 3,212,090 eastbound. Leslie Scott's hectoring continued;

"These lives were lost in three casualties, with the exception of single individuals who were washed overboard. That is the record of the last twenty years."

Curiously, when Scott says that since 1890 there is no evidence of lives having been lost due to an insufficient number of boats, in what manner did, for example, the majority of his 118 fatalities have their lives ended if it was not due to the absence of a lifeboat to make an escape? By drowning in the sea or the effects of hypothermia?

Finsbury M.P. Martin Archer-Shee, an active campaigner over many issues during his time in Parliament, as Sydney Buxton knew full well, particularly on merchant navy matters, commented during the debate:

> "The Hon. Member for Hexham (Scott) talked about boats as if they were not a very necessary part of the equipment of merchant steamers, and yet if he looks at the Report of the Advisory Committee, which has gone very thoroughly into the matter, he will find that ten years ago out of 12,000 men who were saved from ships over 6,000 were saved by the ships' own boats, and in the last ten years half of the men saved from ships have been saved by their own boats. Only in the second decade, no less than 3,000 men were saved by their own boats."

(Lord Mersey's Report HC Deb October 7, 1912, vol 42 cc134)

The noble sacrifice by those gallant men from H.M.S. *Birkenhead* was futile if, as we are invited to believe, every ship that has been wrecked since and many lives lost was not in a major way down to the absence of adequate lifeboats.

On May 9, 1912, in the House of Commons, Liberal M.P. for Lowestoft Sir Edward Beauchamp asked;

> "Whether the President of the Board of Trade can state the number of vessels which have been posted at Lloyds as missing since January 1, to what

nationality they respectively belonged, and the number of lives lost?"

As Chairman of Lloyd's from 1905 to 1913, and vice-chairman from 1915 to 1916, the reasoning behind Sir Edward's question seemed unusual as he could have easily acquired the information himself. Also, he should have known that Lloyd's Register for British and Foreign Shipping does not always include lives lost. Other than having it recorded in the Commons records, there may have been an ulterior motive behind his question.

(Casualty Returns | Archive & Library | Heritage & Education Centre (lrfoundation.org.uk)

Mr Buxton replied;

"I am indebted to the secretary to Lloyds for the following information relating to the vessels posted as missing since January 1 last -

A table was included in the official record.

Nationality.	No. of vessels.	No. of lives lost.
Brazilian	1	7
British (including Colonial)	15	430
French	1	25
German	5	51
Norwegian	4	55
Total	26	568

Sir Edward Beauchamp;

"Arising out of that answer, may I ask my right hon. Friend whether, in the case of missing British vessels, any inquiry was ordered by the Board of Trade?"

Mr. Buxton;
> "Yes; in the case of three small fishing vessels, in which there was no loss of life, and, I think, there was an inquiry into all the cases, but if the hon. Member wants the numbers, and will give me notice, I will endeavour to supply them."

Conservative M.P. Mr Fred Hall (Dulwich) interrupted with what might be construed as a 'loaded' question considering he too was a member of Lloyds and the Baltic Exchange;
> "Is it not the fact that the percentage of British losses is less than the losses of other nationalities, comparing their tonnage with ours?"

Mr Buxton;
> "I gather that will appear from the figures I have read if they are worked out."

(Missing Vessels. HC Deb May 09, 1912, vol 38 cc591-2)

The motivation behind this line of Inquiry remains a mystery in light of the Wreck Commissioners Inquiry, presently underway, not far from Westminster in the Scottish Drill Hall.

A perusal of Lloyd's Register of British and Foreign Shipping for the period January 1 to March 31, 1912, tells us that there were 28 vessels, 14 steamships and 14 sailing vessels, of all nationalities, reported as 'missing' in the same period alluded to in Sydney Buxton's reply. Of these recorded as 'missing,' 7 steamships and three sailing vessels were registered in the U.K. Among the remainder of the sailing vessels, there were 4 Colonial, 1 American, 1 French, 3 German, 1 Italian and 1 Norwegian. The steamships included 1 French, 2 German, 3 Norwegian and 1 Swedish, making a total of 28.

This amounted to a 13,417 grt and 1686 net tonnage loss among 14 British and Colonial vessels and 8,284 grt and 3,285 net tons among 14 Foreign vessels. A figure of 5,133 grt more for those lost from British vessels and 1,599 more net tonnage among foreign vessels reported as missing. The Dulwich M.P. Fred Hall's Inquiry seems misinformed that British and Colonial vessels, although equal in number to those vessels of foreign origins, the overall gross tonnage among the U.K. and Colonial ships lost is greater, not less What is worse is that the President of the Board of Trade appears to agree, in error, with his assumption;

> "*I gather that will appear from the figures I have read if they are worked out.*"

One might conclude that the figures were 'doctored' to make it appear so. It would not be the last time dubious figures for shipping losses would be presented as factual when they were not. One can commiserate when the difficulties of defining between a vessel which is 'lost' and one that is 'missing' is considered, the terminology of Lloyd's Register does not make the task any more straightforward, and the date of losses being reported can often be delayed.

Another chart, constructed from the author's figures taken from Lloyd's Register for the period in question reveals;

Nationality.	No. of vessels.	No. of lives lost.
Brazilian	1	7
British (including Colonial)	14	430
French	2	25
USA	1	?
German	5	51
Italian	1	?
Norwegian	4	55
Swedish	1	?
Total	29	568

Authors Revised Table. Note there are no reliable figures for the total number of lives lost.

There are no Lloyd's listings for Brazilian vessels reported as missing for the period January 1, 1912, to March 31, 1912. There is, however, a listing in the April 1 to 30th June Lloyd's tables for the 248grt vessel *Vista Alegre*, which left Cardiff on January 26 destined for Santos in Brazil with a cargo of coal and was not heard of again. Although Buxton's table lists an unnamed Brazilian vessel and the number of lives lost as 7, Lloyd's has no references to the number of crew onboard the *Vista Alegre*.

It is interesting to note in the President of the Board of Trade's response that he cites figures from Lloyds, not from the Board of Trades' own Casualty Returns. This anomaly contrasts with the shipping losses quoted by Sir Walter Howell and Sir Noman Hill during the British Inquiry, where the Marine Department of the Board of Trade produced records for legal counsel's reference of vessels lost in the North Atlantic for the period 1881-1911.

Lloyd's does not always include in their Register the numbers of lives lost, yet Sydney Buxton mentioned that no lives were lost in three fishing boats that went missing and included in his table is a figure of 568 lives lost, a number his staff could have gleaned from Board of Trade Casualty Returns. Except, we do not know the names of the vessels alluded to, making it difficult to verify accuracy.

Lloyd's list only includes one fishing vessel missing for January 1, 1912, to March 31, 1912, the 171grt *Persian*, which left Grimsby on December 14, 1911, and was not heard of since.

(Casualty Returns | Archive & Library | Heritage & Education Centre (lrfoundation.org.uk)

Under all listings for the period January 1 to March 31, there are 14 other fishing vessels listed. The 148grt Belgian fishing vessel *Isa* was abandoned in the North Sea on January 8, 1912. Similarly, the UK-registered trawler *Svino* was reportedly involved in a collision in the North Sea on February 17, 1912, with the trawler *Lune*. Presumably, the *Lune* remained afloat and could assist the crew of the Grimsby trawler, *Svino*, before she sank. There are no other fishing vessels listed as missing. Most of the remainder were wrecked on various rocks around the coast of the U.K. and listed as such in Lloyd's Register.

According to Buxton's table, losses to British vessels reported as missing for the period January 1, 1912, to March 31, 1912, are listed as 15, although Lloyd's accounts for only 14; 7 of which are steamships with a total tonnage of 12,567 (gross). The remaining British vessels include three sailing vessels totalling 1,686 tons (net). Four Colonial sailing vessels were reported as missing for the same period with a total tonnage of 850 tons (net). Somewhere, according to Buxton's table, one vessel is unaccounted for. Where the 430 lives reported as lost originate, we are left to assume, taken from Board of Trade figures.

O hear us when we cry to Thee,

For those in peril on the sea.

(William Whiting 1860)

The year 1911 witnessed exceptional global weather patterns, bringing higher than average temperatures across the Northern Hemisphere. By early July, in the U.K., drought conditions affected all parts of the country.
(MWR_1911 | Met Office U.A.)

The heat wave and drought ended in mid-September when average temperatures dropped by 20 degrees F (11°C), and the high pressure receded, bringing much-needed rain over all parts of the country. December saw sustained gale force winds reaching Force 10 towards the end of the month.
(www.wrecksite.eu)

The Beaufort Scale in use during that period contains four categories of gale force winds ranging from 7 to 10, which equates to winds at speeds ranging from 39-46 mph (Gale force 7) to 55-63mph (Gale force 10) These winds bring waves reaching 18-25 feet in height to waves of 29-41 feet in height.
(Beaufort wind force scale - Met Office)

The storm took its toll on shipping in the English Channel and the Bay of Biscay area.

For the yearly quarter October 1 to December 31, 1911, for December alone, Lloyd's lists include;
On December 8, 1911, the Norwegian cargo ship S.S. *Goval*, 462grt, departed Blyth with coal to Haugesund and was never seen again. She was presumed lost with all 14 hands.

On December 9, 1911, the French cargo ship *Ville de Carthage*, 1965 grt, on a voyage from Algeria to Dunkirk with a cargo of grain, was abandoned and foundered 90 miles off Ushant at the northernmost edge of the Bay of Biscay. Only five of the 26 on board were rescued with great difficulty by the German steamer *Helen Menzell*.

On December 11, 1911, the British cargo ship *White Rose* departed La Pallice, the commercial deep-water port of La Rochelle, France, for Liverpool with a cargo of wheat and went missing.

The crew of 11 were lost. On September 23 of the same year, an official Inquiry could only determine the most likely cause of the being that;

"Either the cargo shifted and caused the vessel to capsize, or that one of the hatchways was stove in by the heavy sea and the vessel swamped thereby."

On December 14, 1911, the Belgian cargo ship *Flandres*, 2019grt, on a voyage from Newcastle-On-Tyne to Bayonne with 2885 tons of coal, foundered 3 miles northwest from Pointe Argenton, Landunvez. With 25 crew on board, the fate of Captain Christenson and his crew is uncertain.

On December 18, 1911, the British cargo ship *Wingrove*, 2896grt, left Plymouth for Port Said with a cargo of coal, and was reported as missing. She was not heard of ever since. 23 crew were lost. At the official Inquiry into the loss of the *Wingrove*;

> "The actual and immediate cause of the vessel not having been heard of after leaving Plymouth must of necessity, in the circumstances of the case, remain unknown, the Court was of the opinion that the heavy weather prevalent over a wide area after December 18 was sufficient to explain the loss of this ship, as it was undoubtedly the determining factor in the loss of the Hughenden, of the Guillemot, and other steamships at about the same time."

On December 19, 1911, the Norwegian cargo ship S.S. *Vanadis*, 2945grt, was on a voyage from Newcastle on Tyne to Piombino, Italy, with a cargo of coal when she went missing. She was last seen off Ushant at the westernmost tip of Brittany at the northern end of the Bay of Biscay and the entrance to the English Channel. The whole crew, 26 hands in total, were lost.

The worst day that month was Thursday 21, December, when seven vessels were recorded as missing;

The 1754 grt British steamship *Guillemot* on a voyage from the Tyne to Genoa, on December 21, foundered during a gale in the Bay of Biscay. Seven of her crew were rescued by the British S.S. *Lincairn*, although 16 were lost.

On December 21, 1911, the 3342grt German cargo ship *Chios* on a voyage from Hamburg to Oran with a cargo of general and iron, foundered in the Bay of Biscay. No information was available regarding the crew.

Also, on December 21, 1911, the British cargo ship *Hellopes*, 2774grt, on a voyage from Garston to Falmouth with a cargo of coal, suffered a cargo shift in heavy weather near Mount's Bay. The crew of 16 went for the boats before she capsized and foundered.

On December 21, 1911, the Russian dredger *Devolant* 586grt left the Clyde for Odessa. It is surmised she foundered in the English Channel with the loss of her crew of 19 crew.

On December 21, 1911, the Norwegian 1273grt, sailing vessel SV *Carl Bech*, on a voyage from the island group Lobos De Afuera, off the Peruvian coast, to Nantes carrying guano, when was wrecked off Quiberon in the Bay of Biscay. The entire crew of 16 hands were lost.

S.S. *Rafael*, a Uruguayan cargo steamer of 2,340grt which ran aground and was wrecked near Gironde in the Bay of Biscay on December 21, 1911, when on route from West Hartlepool for Bordeaux with a cargo of coal.

While on a voyage from Smyrna to Dublin with a cargo of barley, on December 21, the British steamship *Hughenden*, 3097grt, foundered during a gale. S.S. *Devonshire* picked up only two survivors; possibly 25 were lost.

The British steamer S.S. *Penwith*, 1978 grt on route from Aquilas on December 28 with a crew of 10, was abandoned and foundered in the Bay of Biscay. There are no records of lives lost.

Fourteen vessels were reported missing during that fateful December in 1911. Six were British; the rest were; 1 French, 3 Norwegian, 1 Uruguayan, 1 Russian, 1 German and 1 Belgian. A total of at least 216 lives were lost.

For some, like the 3411grt, U.K. registered sail and steam cargo vessel *Amana* belonging to Furness Withy, which left Leith on December 1, 1911, destined for Philadelphia, and was not heard of since, would not appear on Lloyd's Register until the next quarter, January 1 till March 31, 1912. On board the *Amana*, 31 hands perished with the ship.

Similarly, two weeks previously, the 1178grt German cargo vessel *Friedrich Krupp* went missing on a voyage from Bilbao to Rotterdam on December 16, 1911, with a cargo of iron ore and was not listed in Lloyd's as missing until the following quarter. Bilbao is situated on the southern edge of the Bay of Biscay, and she would have to have crossed the open water at the same time the gale force winds were reported.

Although not connected with the December storms, the fate of another British sail and steam cargo vessel, the 3414grt *Archtor*, when she was reported missing on January 3, 1912, was unknown. She was manned by a crew of 24 persons, all told, including the master's wife, who was on the ship's articles as a stewardess. The official Inquiry in December 1912 concluded;

> "There is no direct evidence as to the cause of the vessel not having been heard of since the pilot left her off Cape Henry on January 3 last, but the probability is that she foundered during the heavy weather which is known to have prevailed in that part of the North Atlantic that she would have to traverse a few days after her departure from Norfolk."

These losses may be small regarding the numbers lost and the vessels' tonnage. However, the Board of Trade owed a duty of care to all British ships plying their trade across the world's oceans. The rules and regulations which governed their safety, construction and operation were intended to protect the seamen from the dangers of shifting cargo and excessive loads, their welfare in terms of conditions onboard and by ensuring the vessel was of a seaworthy state. Failure to enforce these laws and ensure they remained relevant to change were supposed to be the daily bread and butter of the administrators and surveyors employed in ports up and down the country. Any vessel lost at sea with fathers, sons and brothers taken from their families should have cried out for tighter controls and constant vigilance by the authorities to ensure that was the case. Alas, this was evidently not so. Instead, we are left only with the impression of weak attempts at deception and dismissal of these facts by those in a position of responsibility.

Further evidence which tends to support the argument that Lord Mersey may not have had access to the Board of Trade tables especially prepared for the Inquiry, derives from comments made during the Final Arguments when Sir Robert Finlay added;

> "But before calling attention to the evidence as to the uniform practice, I desire to call attention to the fact that it had worked well and given admirable results in practice, and I will test that by taking three sets of tables coming from perfectly different quarters. Will your Lordship take first the table

produced by the Board of Trade? Your Lordship will find it at page 580, Question 22142. These are the statistics produced by the Board of Trade, and they show that;

"From 1892 to 1901, three and a quarter million passengers were carried across the Atlantic, that system of keeping full speed, though ice is reported, being maintained all the time. During that time only 73 were lost. From 1902 to 1911 six million passengers were carried across the Atlantic, that is Question 22148 on the same page, but out of those six millions, only nine were lost."

He continued;

"I very much doubt whether, if the practice of slowing down had been adopted, the loss would not have been very much greater, for a reason I will give presently. The second set of statistics are those of the White Star Line for 11 years. It is on pages 496 and 497.

The first number I am giving is excluding the "Titanic"; 2,179,594 passengers had been carried by the White Star Line during those 11 years. There had been only two deaths from collision. It does not appear it was by icebergs; in fact, I do not think it was, it was by ships. There were only two deaths. How can it be said that there was something wrong with a system which yields such a result as that?"

Sir Robert Finlay continued;

"The statistics do not rest there because you have a third set from Sir Norman Hill. They are framed on a different principle, and they show that there had been 32,000 voyages across the Atlantic in 20 years; that in that time there had been 25 accidents, defining as an accident anything that involved either the loss of life or the loss of the ship, and that in those 25 accidents 68 passengers and 80 crew were lost. That was the total loss on 32,000 voyages."

No one it seems then, or in the decades that have passed since, has paused to ask why there are different sets of figures in the first place and each offered up as *bona fide* shipping figures. There can only be one set of accurate figures. Yet, Sir Robert Finlay is allowed to badger the Court with innuendo dressed up as facts.

The 'smoking gun' in the narrative presented, when Sir Robert Finlay drew Lord Mersey's attention to figures already in evidence, i.e., the transcript of those earlier statements from Sanderson, Hill, and Howell, not the information compiled in the Board of Trade's own tables, from which the information had likely been taken, he was legitimising the evidence submitted by the witnesses and not the figures listed in the Board of Trade Tables. By not entering the 'official' Tables into evidence, there is no authentic source from which to make comparisons.

This was the surreptitious intention in getting each of these witnesses to state, on record, selected shipping figures during their testimony whereby Messrs. Finlay, Butler-Aspinall and Sir Rufus Isaacs could quote them as statements of fact in their summations. By not submitting the source of the actual figures into evidence, the lie becomes the truth and hey, presto! as if by magic, no one sees the smoke and mirrors deception in plain sight before their eyes.

It seems not even Sir Robert Finlay paused to consider why the figures he was quoting and submitted as evidence conflicted with material provided by the Board of Trade. Why Sir Robert Finlay was stating that; "*There had been only two deaths from collision. It does not appear it was by icebergs; in fact, I do not think it was, it was by ships.*" he did not think it was due to icebergs when it was well known that it was a collision with the *Florida* and the resulting rescue became a cause célèbre for an enthralled public is a mystery.

In his dogged pursuit of a verdict in his client's favour, Counsel for the White Star Line may also have been sailing his own particular defence 'close to the wind' in enticing Harold Sanderson, to lie under oath.* "*And is that the whole amount of loss of life which took place in that number of passengers carried? - Yes, it is.*" he asked the witness. And perpetuating the lie, "*There had been only two deaths from collision*" in his final arguments. It is a discussion for another day to consider whether White Star counsel was guilty of suborning perjury when it was shown that Sir Robert Finlay and Harold Sanderson knew that figure, was incorrect. During the Inquiry there were so many abuses of legal procedures it appears one more would not make much difference. Although the prospect of penal servitude for the perpetrators seems fitting.

*The Perjury Act of 1911. CHAPTER 6 1 and 2 Geo 5
1 Perjury.
(1) If any person lawfully sworn as a witness or as an interpreter in a judicial proceeding wilfully makes a statement

material in that proceeding, which he knows to be false or does not believe to be true, he shall be guilty of perjury, and shall, on conviction thereof on indictment, be liable to penal servitude for a term not exceeding seven years, or to imprisonment . . . F1 for a term not exceeding two years, or to a fine or to both such penal servitude or imprisonment and fine

(2) The expression "judicial proceeding" includes a proceeding before any court, tribunal, or person having by law power to hear, receive, and examine evidence on oath.
(www.legislation.gov.uk)

The same Board of Trade figures stated clearly that three passengers died from *Republic* due to the collision, not the two he repeated. Unabashed, he drove forward undeterred by the contradiction.

"Surely," he said, "by the light of experience, by the light of these figures, the three sets of statistics from different quarters, one sees that it is under all normal circumstances possible to see an iceberg in time to avoid it, and that this accident must have been the result, as I hope to satisfy the Court beyond all reasonable doubt, of an extraordinary combination of circumstances, and that there was not any fault of any kind on the part of Captain Smith. I submit there was not even an error of judgment. Negligence, I submit, is out of the question, and cannot be found in face of the evidence which I am going to call attention to with regard to the uniform practice. Error of judgment, I submit, there was none because a man does not commit an error of judgment because he does something which in the result is followed by unfortunate consequences. A man may do the rashest possible thing, and the consequences may be most beneficial, but he is rash all the same; a man may do the wisest possible thing and the results may be disastrous, but he was wise all the same. One cannot judge by the result which happened in the particular case as to the wisdom or unwisdom of the course taken. My very respectful submission is that negligence there certainly was none, and that there was not even an error of judgment, but that Captain Smith acted rightly in following the usual course."

Sir Robert Finlay mentions the "*uniform practice*" of twenty years where he conveniently ignored only the marginal increase in speed compared with the two-fold increase in size of Trans-Atlantic passenger vessels over the same period.

A previous command of Smith's before the *Titanic* was the 24,679 grt vessel *Adriatic* which was 729 feet long and had a cruising speed of 19 knots. Almost half as heavy as *Titanic* and well over a hundred feet shorter in length. Smith could hardly be said to have gained enough service time on 'Olympic class' vessels to believe he had acquired experience to know how she would handle a crisis requiring emergency evasive action. A fact tragically put to the test on the night of April 14, 1912.

Sir Robert Finlay goes on;

"The whole importance of the matter is when one comes to translate the general proposition, which your Lordship justly characterised as a truism, into practice. The practical question is, can you in clear weather see a berg in time to avoid it? And the answer I say is demonstrated, by the experience of

20 years, to be that you can; and the answer to the question, "How did the "Titanic" not see it in time?" is supplied by the fact that the circumstances were extraordinary and abnormal, and such as may never occur again."

The Commissioner:
"You have not overlooked the fact that this was what you might call an abnormal ship. She was a very long ship, and a very big ship, and the circle in which she could turn was a large one."

Sir Robert Finlay: "Yes, my Lord."

The Commissioner: "It was not easy for that ship to turn a circle which would enable her to avoid anything in front of her."

Sir Robert Finlay: "She was a big ship, undoubtedly."

The Commissioner: "And that was a circumstance known to the Captain."

At this point White Star counsel appears to plumb the depths of nonsensical argument when he conveniently introduces the spurious example of making comparisons with other shipping lines. Except other shipping lines were not the ones facing a tribunal.

Sir Robert Finlay;
"But your Lordship recollects there were a great many other ships not very much less. I forget the lengths* of the "Lusitania" and the "Mauretania," but they are not very far short. For all practical purposes, I do not suppose there is much difference."

(*787ft and 739.5ft. The Titanic was 883ft)

However, to illustrate the point Cunard's RMS *Lusitania* at 31,550 grt was 96.5 feet shorter in length and comfortable at a service speed of 24 knots. For comparison, baseball fans would likely know the distance from the pitcher's mound to the edge of the outfield grass, just beyond second base, is 95 feet. Even simpler, a ten-storey building comes in at roughly 100 feet.

Lord Mersey understood the general principle of the longer the ship, the greater the turning circle. Sir Robert Finlay was grasping at straws in his desperate claims. In reality, the Cunard's vessels benefitted from the input of naval architects from the Admiralty, who had introduced refinements to her hull profile and rudder to improve the vessel's turning response further.

The Commissioner:

"I am told they were about 90 ft. shorter* than the "Titanic."

*(Actually 96ft. As an example. A tennis court is 78 feet in length. The *Mayflower* was about 90 feet in length.)

Sir Robert Finlay:

"That does not make very much difference. Then your Lordship recollects the great big German liners. It is not as if this were a new departure altogether. This was a gradual growth; it had been going on."

Kronprinz William was 663ft. *Kaiser Wilhelm der Grosse* was 655ft. *Kronprinzessin Cecilie* 706ft, all considerably shorter in length. With that Finlay dismisses the valid point raised by Lord Mersey.

On Day 34 of the Final Arguments, the Attorney-General noted;
> "Therefore, what we have got established is that this vessel going along at this pace, travelling at this, 700 yards a minute, only sees the iceberg at a distance of 466 yards and that that is not enough."

He added; "*However quickly the men may act at the helm, however swiftly the order is given, and however quickly the Officer in charge acts, you cannot navigate that vessel with her 850 feet length* out of the way of that iceberg in time.*" (Authors Italics)

*(Actually 883ft)

The Attorney-General stated authoritatively;
> "In the statements which I have been making in regard to these matters, I think I am stating facts proved on the evidence which are beyond all question and beyond all controversy."

Even today, the dismissive arrogance demonstrated by White Star counsel defies belief. We cannot simply accept that Sir Robert Finlay was either poorly briefed or was ignoring the historical evidence, stating dismissively, "*That (length) does not make very much difference.*" Ships regularly had incidents involving icebergs, but few suffered serious harm, primarily due to reduced speed and shorter length. None of this is rebuked by Lord Mersey, who raised the question initially, for Sir Robert Finlay's flippant comments. Even the Attorney-General's definitive statement, "*you cannot navigate that vessel with her 850 feet length out of the way of that iceberg in time,*" is disregarded in the muddle of semantics created by the White Star counsel.

Writer Joseph Conrad, who spent many years at sea, albeit on smaller vessels was qualified to comment;
"In reading the reports, the first reflection which occurs to one is that, if that luckless ship had been a couple of hundred feet shorter, she would probably gone clear of the danger. But then, perhaps, she could not have had a swimming bath and a French Café."

(Notes on Life and Letters Joseph Conrad, Some Reflections On The Loss Of The Titanic – 1912. p213-228. DoubleDay, Page & Company 1921. p 219)

Any 'growlers' snapping at the steel plates of the *Titanic* were very different from the real-life crocodiles lurking in the disease-ridden Congo rivers of Conrad's experience.

Growlers are smaller fragments of ice and are roughly the size of a small truck or grand piano. They extend less than three feet above the sea surface and occupy an area of about 215 square feet.

(https://oceanservice.noaa.gov/about/faq.html)

While it might be said that both men shared the same profession, each taking the Board of Trade examinations and gaining a master's ticket, their experiences were very different. Conrad, it would appear, used much of his experiences at sea as the source for many of his novels and gritty views of humankind.

There is no doubt that Conrad's previous experience at sea provided him with a vast pool of colourful and interesting characters for his works of fiction. This also worked in his favour when he presented his observations in the form of his 'Notes on Life and Letters.'

Coming some years after he had left the sea, his unique insights into the debate that transpired following the *Titanic* disaster served as a necessary purgative to the excesses of sentimentality and attempts at mythicising the *Titanic* story by the Press and the public at large. Conrad exploited his experience of his time as a sailor. He wrote at times with sardonic prose that served to topple egos and arrogance and, in his singular way, spelt out his concerns regarding the urgency with which the shipping industry was embracing new, untried technology as a solution to the risks involved in the pursuit of profit at the expense of safety.

Conrad's views on the entitled individuals of the Board of Trade were no less critical;

> "An office with adequate and no doubt comfortable furniture and a lot of perfectly irresponsible gentlemen, who exist packed in its equable atmosphere softly, as if in cottonwool, and with no care in the world; for there can be no care without personal responsibility – such, for instance, as seamen have – those seamen from whose mouths this irresponsible institution can take away the bread – as a disciplinary measure."

(Notes on Life and Letters Joseph Conrad, Some Reflections On The Loss Of The Titanic – 1912. p213-228. DoubleDay, Page & Company 192. P 216.)

Sir Robert Finlay had also said, "*That* (length) *does not make very much difference. Then your Lordship recollects the great big German liners.*"

The North German Lloyd passenger liner *Kron Prinz Wilhelm* narrowly avoided a serious collision with an iceberg off the Grand Banks when she spotted an iceberg ahead and took avoiding action. Details in the report states that there was violent contact made, and it was primarily due to the vessel's reduced speed and at 663 feet in length, 220 feet less than the *Titanic*, that a more serious incident was avoided.

(New York Times, July 11, 1907)

One example of how lower speed and shorter length played a part in saving the vessel.

Sir Robert Finlay: "I only refer to it in a casual way at this moment for the purpose of showing how the lengths went on gradually increasing. You have the "Adriatic" and the "Baltic," (both 729ft) and then finally you have the "Titanic" and the "Olympic." (both 883ft) That increase in size (18%) was gradual, but side by side with that growth in White Star vessels despite Finlay's claims, this 'growth' was not commensurate with White Star's rivals. At over 90 feet less in length, the Cunarders *Mauretania* and *Lusitania* were commissioned in 1907, the same year White Star and Harland and Wolfe are said to have proposed the construction of the 'Olympic- class' vessels. Sir Robert Finlay went on;

> "*I quite appreciate the point, but I submit to your Lordship that there is nothing in the additional length of the "Titanic" to render it improper to adhere to the ordinary practice which had always been pursued in this matter.*" (Authors Italics)

That Sir Robert Finlay was never corrected in his claims provides further evidence that Lord Mersey and his 'expert' advisers went along with his remarks unchallenged. The preponderance of vessels that were increasing in great leaps of size were those mostly commissioned by White Star.

The Commissioner:

> "I should have thought that the great length of this ship might make a difference, whether considerable or not, I cannot say, in the difficulty of avoiding an object."

Again, the assessors should have advised Lord Mersey on this point. Clearly, the 154-foot increase in length and the additional tonnage above Smith's earlier commands make nonsense out of Finlay's claim that "*there is nothing in the additional length of the "Titanic" to render it improper to adhere to the ordinary practice*," especially when the *Titanic* lay at the bottom of the Atlantic Ocean.

Sir Robert Finlay:

> "My Lord, is not the answer with reference to any suggestion of negligence that may be made on that score supplied by the fact that there are other ships, which, for practical purposes, are as big, which have adhered to the same practice?"

Again, Finlay attempts to befuddle the narrative by invoking in his client's defence what White Star's rivals practiced. However, Captain Smith was never master of a rival's vessel. The figures above disprove Sir Robert Finlay's assertions that competitor's vessels were keeping pace with White Star's construction of new vessels. For "*practical purposes*," the length of a vessel is a factor in her ability to avoid obstacles ahead. Sir Robert Finlay finishes by saying;

> "It is a matter which I suggest cannot be imputed as negligence to any Officer in charge of the vessel that he did not vary from the ordinary practice in a way which no other Commander in charge of

vessels which were approximately the same length, not very much shorter, did."

The inescapable fact remained, "*No other Commander in charge of vessels*" struck an iceberg in the North Atlantic, which caused them to sink.

If it was not negligence, then it was recklessness compounded by ignorance of the handling characteristics of 'Olympic – class' vessels and probably, the failure to appreciate the enormous suction effect of these vessels on nearby objects and the distance required to spot an iceberg in her path in time to take avoiding action.

A 1909 pilot's guide supplied to all ships stated.

"*One of the chief dangers in crossing the Atlantic lies in the probability of encountering masses of ice, in the form of both icebergs and extensive fields of solid compact sea ice. Ice is more likely to be encountered in this route between April and August, both months inclusive, than at other times.*" (Authors Italics)

The year 1912 saw the heaviest ice for any April in the new century, a record that stood until 1972.

(Icebergs in the North Atlantic Ocean | National Geographic Society)

G.K. Chesterton wrote.

"The very lines of the boat have the swift poetry of peril; the very carriage and gestures of the boat are those of a thing assailed. But if you make your boat so large that it does not even look like a boat, but like a sort of watering-place, it must, by the deepest habit of human nature, induce a less vigilant attitude of the mind."

(G.K. Chesterton; Illustrated London News, May 11, 1912)

It is worth noting that Sir Robert Finlay's soporific closing arguments took almost three days to complete. Although regarded by some as a brilliant jurist, he was not in the prime of his life when asked by the White Star Line to be their advocate during the investigation into the loss of their flagship liner. That he exploited every reason, plausible or otherwise, he could conceive in defence of his clients can be found in his interminable closing speech. A speech during which he received great latitude from Lord Mersey.

It could be said that the relative success Sir Robert Finlay enjoyed when Lord Mersey found no cause to blame *Titanic*'s Captain, Edward Smith, and by default, his clients, White Star, from any guilt by association, was less to do with his legal brilliance and more to do with an accommodating opposing counsel and a compliant Wreck Commissioner.

Thirty-six years before the sinking of the *Titanic*, confirmation can be found that the processes involved in inquiries into shipping losses were very much open to the interpretation of the appointed Wreck Commissioner. On July 27th, 1876, the British barque *Dinorah*, on a voyage from the Tyne to Brindisi on the Adriatic coast with a cargo of coal, sank after a collision with the steamer SS *Dorunda*, 35 miles east of Gibraltar, where ten people lost their lives. In setting out his stall before the subsequent inquiry began the newly appointed Wreck Commissioner, H.C. Rothery stated;

> "*An impression seems to prevail that those inquiries must be regarded as in the nature of a criminal proceeding, and that they must, consequently, be governed by the rules which prevail*

in such cases. I cannot, however, concur in that opinion."
(Authors Italics)
(The Wreck Commissioner, in the case of the "Dinorah" and "Dorunda." October 30th, 1876)

The suggestion being that the formal etiquette of Jurisprudence would be more relaxed and informal and vulnerable to misuse. A feature that would recur in other inquiries and in 1912, colour the events in the Scottish Drill Hall and cause controversy thereafter. Another consequence of a Wreck Commissioners Inquiry taking the form of a 'non-adversarial' nature.

Considering the Prime Minister, no less in response to a question in Parliament stated;

"The interests of the general public will be specially represented by the Law Officers of the Crown and Counsel appearing with them at the Inquiry."
(Board Of Trade (Marine Department). Hc Deb May 06, 1912, Vol 38 Cc41-4)

Although incisive and candid, Sir Rufus Isaacs's closing arguments were moribund in comparison. Sir Robert Finlay went on;

"Every one of these vessels had been keeping up speed after ice was reported, and yet I gather the Attorney-General is going to ask the Court to find negligence on the part of the captain of the "Titanic" for doing what every Captain during all that time had done."

Perhaps if the Attorney-General had been more animated and vocal, Lord Mersey might have had difficulty in by-passing the blatant simplicity of the Attorney-General's lucid arguments.

> *"However quickly the men may act at the helm, however swiftly the order is given, and however quickly the Officer in charge acts, you cannot navigate that vessel with her 850 feet length out of the way of that iceberg in time.*" (Authors Italics)

Whatever else White Star counsel could conjure up by way of mitigation, not every Captain could run headlong into an iceberg close to the size of Rockall in the North Atlantic and escape his day of reckoning.

One contemporary writer recognised it for what it was;

> "The one thing positively known was that Captain Smith had lost his ship by deliberately and knowingly steaming into an icefield at the highest speed he had coal for. He paid the penalty; so, did most of those for whose lives he was responsible. Had he brought them and the ship safely to land, nobody would have taken the smallest notice of him."

(George Bernard Shaw; Some Unmentioned Morals. May 14, 1912, The Daily News and Leader)

It would take the supreme efforts of a few determined lawyers and relatives to persevere the following year, against the odds, by taking the Oceanic Steam Navigation Company, effectively, the White Star Line, to the Royal Courts of Justice in London, before Judge Bailhache. There, a special jury would find Captain Edward Smith, belatedly, guilty of negligence, too little fanfare, or public indignation. A judgement Lord Mersey had, many believed, avoided delivering, with much the same evidence and testimony from the previous year. Despite the protestations of White Star counsel and an Appeal in November 1913, the test case of an elderly Irish cattle farmer, who had lost a son in the sinking, was upheld by another High Court Judge, Lord Vaughan-Williams, to ram home the implications of one man's actions, who on that night, drove his vessel towards disaster. Undeterred, the White Star Line, in the guise of its parent company, brought the case before the House of Lords, where they presumably hoped the powerful shipping interests represented there would help them carry the day. However, this was not to be. The Court judged the grounds of appeal were without merit, and the appeal was dismissed in February the following year. The delayed verdict of negligence in the navigation of the *Titanic* through excessive speed in an area of known ice was upheld. Liability and reparations would finally be settled in 1915 in the U.S. Courts, and even then, stubbornly resisted by representatives of White Star to the bitter end.

In a seemingly contrary argument in his closing statement, Sir Robert Finlay offered his explanation;

> "Now, my Lord, there is a very good reason indeed why they should not slow down when in the neighbourhood of icebergs, and it is this, that you are apt to have fog coming on when you are among icebergs, and if the fog comes on when you are among icebergs it is a very dangerous thing indeed."

Sir Robert Finlay, it appeared, had unwittingly given the court insight into routine seafaring practice in fog.

The Commissioner:

> "But is it? If you are in a fog and you are conscious that there are icebergs about, why cannot you stop?"

Sir Robert Finlay: "Of course, you would have to stop."

The Commissioner:

"I have been told that they do go ahead as quickly as they can sometimes through a fog; that is, I suppose, for the purpose of getting through the fog and out of it?"

Further on the Commissioner queried;

"Suppose you do become involved in a fog among icebergs, then you would have to stop altogether? I do not know then that would deliver you from all danger of accident; if you have these icebergs drifting about and coming grinding up against your vessel, I do not know that you would be immune from damage even in that case."

A week after disaster struck the *Titanic* in the North Atlantic, on April 24, the Canadian Pacific passenger liner *Empress of Britain* with 1,460 passengers on board, struck an iceberg 250 miles from the reported position *Titanic* went down. The vessel was going slowly at the time due to dense fog. The account told of the lookout alerting the bridge and the engines being reversed but there was contact made with the iceberg, but no serious damage occurred.

(New York Times April 27, 1912)

The actions of the master of the *Empress of Britain* disavowed Finlay's argument in favour of a vessel's speed through fog. The actions of one captain probably saved the lives of his passengers and crew the procrastination of the other captain, we know, did not. This all took place a mere seven days after the commencement of the U.S. Senate hearings and one week prior to the start of the British Inquiry. The entourage of lawyers, pressmen, witnesses, and members of the public who commuted daily to the U.S. hearings could not have helped but have read in the Saturday-morning editions of yet another heart-stopping incident involving a large passenger liner at sea. The coverage made the front page of the New York Times. Over their morning coffee, this news should have made them more resolute in their determination to get to the truth of the *Titanic*.

In contrast to the pleadings of White Star counsel and if further evidence were needed of the reckless practice by ships captains of maintaining speed in adverse weather, on May 16, while the British Inquiry was still ongoing, Sir Clement Kinloch-Cooke (Unionist M.P. Devonport) asked the President of the Board of Trade, Sydney Buxton in the House of Commons if;

> "He will give the number of casualties found to be due to vessels travelling at a high rate of speed in fog, mist, falling snow, or heavy rainstorms by inquiries held by the Board of Trade during the last ten years?"

Mr Buxton produced a table which he explained listed;

> "The number of cases in which Courts of Inquiry into Shipping Casualties in the United Kingdom have found that the vessels concerned were navigated at too great a rate of speed in thick weather."

Year	Fog	Mist	Snow	Rain	Total
1902	1	2	-	-	3
1903	8	-	-	-	8
1904	5	4	-	-	9
1905	4	2	2	-	8
1906	8	4	-	2	14
1907	9	-	1	-	10
1908	5	4	-	-	9
1909	4	1	2	1	8
1910	8	1	-	1	10
1911	7	-	1	-	8
1912	2	1	-	-	3
Total	**61**	**19**	**6**	**4**	**90**

(Table reproduced from the original)

There was no further elaboration from Mr Buxton as to the time of year or the location of these incidents. Nonetheless, the table revealed that in the period 1902-1912, no less than 90 cases were shown to have resulted from *"navigating at too great a rate of speed."*

No fewer than 61 of that number in fog, supposedly to be among the most feared conditions encountered by ship's captains.

At that point Sir Clement asked the President of the Board of Trade whether he will consider the;

"Advisability of amending Article 16 of the regulations for preventing collisions at sea, setting out that every vessel shall, in a fog, mist, falling snow, or heavy rainstorms, go at a moderate speed, having careful regard to existing circumstances, to ensure similar care is taken when a vessel is in the vicinity of icebergs?"

Mr Buxton replied;

"The hon. Member's suggestion shall receive my very careful consideration. He is doubtless aware, however, that international consent is required for any alteration in the Collision Regulations."

(HC Deb May 16, 1912, vol 38 c1438W)

The Board of Trade, when all is said and done, it seemed, did a lot of "*careful consideration*" and, regrettably, stands accused of doing very little in the way of positive action.

"There be dragons..."

During Sir Robert Finlay's exhaustive closing arguments, Lord Mersey, the Wreck Commissioner, asked: "Are there many cases reported of collisions with icebergs?"
To which counsel for the White Star Line replied dismissively "Very few, my Lord."
The Commissioner continued: "I think there are very few indeed."
Sir Robert Finlay, of course, agreed; "Very few," he reiterated. A disingenuous reply from the scheming White Star counsel. Had he been more forthcoming, he might have admitted that there were certainly numerous incidents of collisions with icebergs, many with serious damage, although few with loss of life. It was not in his client's best interests to have this aspect of the Inquiry opened for examination.
The Commissioner went on;
> "There was one a good many years ago. To which Finlay said: "The "Arizona" I think your Lordship is referring to."

On November 7, 1879, the Guion-owned passenger steamship S.S. *Arizona* suffered a collision with an iceberg en route to Liverpool. While the damage was severe, she remained afloat and was able to proceed to St. John's, NF., where she underwent temporary repairs before returning to her original builder's yard on the River Clyde for repairs. The cause of the accident, it was discerned, was the failure to keep a proper lookout. An accusation that was also pertinent to the *Titanic*.

The Commissioner enquired: "Is that the only one?"

Sir Robert Finlay: "I think that is the only reported case, as far as I know."

The Commissioner added: "I mean a reported case." Sir Robert Finlay, obviously uncertain of where the Commissioner was taking his line of enquiries, replied: "It will be in the early eighties."

The Commissioner stated: "This is 1880."

In an attempt to steer the Inquiry back on course, the Attorney-General interjected: "Of course, you could not get the ordinary collision action; you have that difficulty." The "*collision action*" the Attorney-General was referring to was presumably a "side-on" event where one vessel strikes the other by the bow, not the "head-on" mechanism of a collision with an iceberg or other obstacle in the vessel's path.

The Commissioner conceded: "That is so." It seems both the Attorney-General and counsel for White Star were becoming increasingly apprehensive with the Commissioner's dalliances with ships colliding with icebergs. Sir Robert Finlay said in response;

"Not in rem (sic) against an iceberg."

(*in rem*. Adj. from the Latin *"against or about a thing"*)

Not prepared to abandon this line of inquisition just yet, the Commissioner stated:

"But there have been a very large number of Wreck Enquiries, and I was wondering whether any wreck had been reported where the cause of the wreck was collision with an iceberg."

Suggesting signs of impatience or irritation at the Commissioner's persistence, Sir Robert Finlay said, "I am not aware of any Wreck Enquiry under such circumstances."

The Commissioner: "Then such an accident as this is of very rare occurrence, I should think."

In reply, Sir Robert Finlay reveals a certain amount of relief:

"Yes, and of course, my Lord, that is one of the circumstances to which I appeal, as showing that the practice that has always been pursued is a reasonable practice."

However, White Star counsel had not steered his own particular vessel into calmer waters. Joseph Cotter, founder of the Ships' Stewards, Cooks, Butchers, and Bakers Union, to give it its full title, himself a former Cunard steward and now secretary of the Union and representing those crewmen from the *Titanic* had something to say on the matter.

The Union played a prominent part in the Seamen's Strike of 1911, working closely with other seamen unions to obtain grudging recognition by the ship owner's cabal, the Shipping Federation. Cotter had a reputation for his passionate speeches and impetuous temperament and was, nicknamed "Explosive Joe."

(*The Seamen*: A History of the National Union of Seamen. Marsh, Arthur; Ryan, Victoria. Malthouse Press, Oxford (1989). pp. 113–115.)

This interruption might have been viewed as antagonistic, not least to Lord Mersey, himself known to be short on tolerance of seamen's union representatives, but mostly to the Attorney-General and especially Sir Robert Finlay.

Cotter, it seems, was unwilling to sit by and allow White Star counsel to ride roughshod over the history of collisions with icebergs. He said, "There have been heaps of collisions with icebergs, my Lord, but not wrecks."

The Attorney-General replied tersely: "Yes, certainly."

Gauging from the absence of any response from opposing counsel, it perhaps indicates that Cotter had hit home with his comment. Cotter went on;

> "The "Lake Champlain" only last year, was in collision; the "Arizona" was in collision, and several have been in collision."

Conceding the point, the Commissioner enquired: "Are not those cases reported anywhere?"

Of course, Cotter knew the answer: "The Board of Trade will have the facts, my Lord."

Counsel for the White Star Line we know would already have had access to the Board of Trade's records of shipping losses and would have desired to steer attention away from any entries which might conflict with their strategy of wilful ignorance. For Sir Robert Finlay to have declared "*as far as I know*" as an excuse when the court was speculating about the number of incidents involving icebergs demonstrated that this was a subject, he found particularly uncomfortable. He knew exactly the record of casualties at sea involving ice; he did not want the court to know that it was indeed more common than Lord Mersey knew. Had that remained the case, Finlay and Sir Rufus Isaacs would have been satisfied that Lord Mersey "*should think*" it was a rare occurrence.

We know the Board of Trade did indeed produce shipping records for the Inquiry. They show that the 20 years ended June 30, 1911; there were 17 collisions, of which 12 resulted in the total loss of the vessel, 7 of which resulted in the loss of 12 lives. However, the tables do not specify the nature of the collisions. Of the 211 cases listed in the Board of Trade documents of vessels lost due to "*other causes*," no fewer than 11 are reported as an encounter with ice. Other losses reported as "*missing*" also raises the possibility of collisions with icebergs or some other derelict, undetected, semi-submerged and lying-in wait for the unwary skipper.

In an attempt to recover, Sir Robert Finlay stated: "There was no loss of life in the "Lake Champlain" Mr Cotter replied, "No, but she was in collision; she struck an iceberg."

Sir Robert Finlay: "Did she do any damage?" Mr Cotter: "Yes, she bent in her bows."

The former Beaver Line's *Lake Champlain*, which in 1901, was bound from Liverpool to Montreal on May 6, with over 1,000 passengers on board with a top speed of 13 knots was forced to head to St John's, Newfoundland for essential repairs. Incidentally, *Lake Champlain* was the first recorded merchant ship to be equipped with wireless telegraphy.

(Ships of the World An Historical Encyclopedia, 1995)

Earlier, during the Inquiry, *Titanic* stewardess Annie Robinson was asked by Mr Cotter when giving evidence before Lord Mersey;

"Have you ever been in a collision before?" - Yes.
What ship was that? The "Lake Champlain?" - Yes.
Also, an iceberg? - Yes.
So that you knew exactly what to do on this occasion? - Yes.
And you, did it? - Yes."
(Brit Inq13306-10)

This brief exchange suggests there was enough concern by the *Lake Champlain*'s captain to order preparedness for evacuation.

Sir Robert Finlay appeared to dismiss this information as irrelevant.

"Still, the fact remains that there have been extremely few, and the absence of casualties is what the Table shows."

The "Table" of course, would only show what the White Star counsel wanted to reveal, and those adulterated numbers would remain in the mind of the Commissioner after the exchange.

One possible explanation why the Attorney-General remained non-committal during this exchange was offered during his summation when Sir Rufus Isaacs took the opportunity to refute claims made by Sir Robert Finlay regarding incidents involving collisions with ice.

"Now collision with an iceberg is a well-known danger of navigation. Your Lordship asked a question which, at the time, we were unable to answer, as to whether there were any reported cases which dealt with collisions with icebergs, and you were referred to the "Arizona". My Lord, there is another - I only mention it in answer to what was put by your Lordship - there was the "Cretic" in 1891, *which was the subject of another Enquiry, with regard to a vessel which had come into collision with an iceberg. There was no lookout; that was what was found as the cause."

_(British Wreck Commissioner's Inquiry Day 34 Final Arguments)

Launched on the Tyne by Leslie & Co., February 25, 1902, as the "*Hanoverian*" for Frederick Leyland & Co. (the Leyland Line). When International Mercantile Marine bought out both Leyland and Dominion lines, the *Hanoverian* was transferred to Dominion and renamed the "*Mayflower*". Later the same year, the vessel was transferred to the White Star Line and renamed *Cretic*.

_(www.titanicinquiry.org/ships/cretic.php)

Given the plethora of such incidents, a half-hearted rebuttal from a learned jurist amounted to nothing more than a poor attempt to recover the initiative. The official transcript appears to be in error as Sir Rufus Isaacs mentions an incident with the *Cretic*, which was not built until 1902 and should have read as the *Critic*, which was involved in a collision with ice near the Grand Banks on March 16, 1891.

_(British Wreck Commissioner's Inquiry Day 34 Final Arguments)

Little is known about the Allan Lines vessel or the incident except that she appears to have been able to continue her return trip to Leith with her cargo of flour damaged due to the ingress of water.

(newicedata.com)
A mistake that might have been made with the reputed poor acoustics in the Scottish Drill Hall. Nonetheless, had the Attorney-General been better informed and motivated to score points over his opposite counsel, he could have used the opportunity and gained an advantage. In that, he might also have been badly let down by his staff researchers. It is not that there were so few incidents available to choose from.

As mentioned previously, the loss of the Liverpool steamer *Amana* in December 1911 resulted in such an inquiry. The report of the Inspector Captain W. A. Faucett stated the *Amana* was built in 1895 and she was constructed of steel with seven watertight bulkheads to the height of the spar deck. Fitted with a cellular double bottom, the general reports from the master and officers showed that she was seaworthy in every respect and in good order.

The official Inquiry determined;

> "The cause of the loss of the "Amana" the inspector declares, is impossible of definite solution and must remain a matter of uncertainty but was probably due to collision with an iceberg or a derelict. Very bad weather prevailed in the North Atlantic early in December, and she may have succumbed to a heavy sea."

It was also stated that icebergs were reported in the track of the *Amana*, only adds to the suggestion that she could easily have struck an iceberg or a derelict.

(Wrecksite - Amana Cargo Ship 1895-1911)

Except Sir Robert Finlay would not have countenanced anything other than a large passenger-carrying steamship relevant to his pleadings on behalf of the White Star Line dismissing the lives of the *Amand's* 31 crew members.

During the decades 1840 -1870, there were approximately 63 incidents recorded where vessels are presumed to have been lost, damaged, or foundered following a collision with ice. Many appear to have been due to having their bows stoved in or lost rigging; in many cases, their wooden planks unable to resist the crushing forces and sprung leaks. Some were able to continue into port for repairs; and some disappeared without a trace. The *William Brown* incident in April 1841 became notorious mainly for what occurred after the vessel foundered in rough seas after striking an iceberg. Of 83 crew and passengers, 33 went down with the ship; the remainder took to boats. Later testimony revealed 17 passengers were thrown overboard to lighten No 1 boat, which was later picked up by the *Crescent*.

The period began with the loss of 120 from the *President* and ended with the loss of the *City of Boston* in January 1870 on the eastbound voyage from Halifax to Liverpool. She had 191 people on board: 55 cabin passengers, 52 steerage passengers and a crew of 84. She never reached her destination, and no indisputable trace of her was ever found. The *City of Boston* became the largest vessel of its time to disappear without a trace off the coast of Nova Scotia. She had stopped at Halifax for mail, coal, and passengers on her regular New York to Liverpool route. Reports that a violent gale and snowstorm took place two

days after her departure, which may have been the cause of the wreck; alternatively, it may have been a collision with an iceberg. The disaster had serious effects on the Inman Line as it was the fifth major loss to their fleet.
(Loss of City of Boston, Halifax to Liverpool, 1870 (archive.org))

There were notable losses in 1854, which recorded the greatest loss of 480 souls from the *City of Glasgow* when she was lost without a trace on a voyage from Liverpool to Philadelphia. Two years later, the *John Rutledge* was abandoned when the bow was holed after she struck an iceberg, and there was only one survivor from 119 passengers and crew. The *Pacific* went down with all hands in January 1856, her fate described by a message allegedly found in a bottle washed up in the Hebrides. In the space of eight weeks in early 1856, four vessels were lost: the steamship Pacific, the *John Rutledge* and two fully rigged clipper ships, the *Driver*, and the *Ocean Queen*.

The *Driver* had sailed from Liverpool on February 12, 1856, with a crew of 22 men and six officers, together with 344 passengers. She was not heard of since. There is evidence to support the belief that the *Ocean Queen* was lost in the same ice, which also claimed the steamer *Pacific* and the clipper *John Rutledge* as well as the *Driver*. An estimated 830 lives were lost due to ice in the North Atlantic among those vessels alone.

In those decades, for many of the other reports, the outcome is unknown, and the number of lives lost is not recorded.
(http://www.icedata.ca/Pages/ShipCollisions/ShipCol_OnlineSearch.php)
(Wrecksite - Driver Clipper 1854-1856)

(The John Rutledge Shipwreck: A Horrifying Ordeal and One Miraculous Survival - New England Historical SocietyWreck site.)

The years 1871–1880 saw an increase in the reporting of the number of vessels in collision with ice numbering about 72, reflecting perhaps the increase in shipping volume. Notable also is the reduction in the number of lives lost, which was counted in single figures, possibly due to the increase in the use of iron hulls, buying precious time, in some instances, for the passengers and crew to escape. There were two notable exceptions; the Dominion Lines 2,484 grt *Vicksburg* in June 1875, where 47 were lost, including the captain. In 1880, the 1232-ton *Edith Troop* built in 1872 and registered in St John N.B. en route from New Orleans to Calais was reported missing in ice and presumed sunk with the loss of the crew of 25.

The British Inquiry heard about the incident involving the *Arizona*, which, on November 7, 1879, while she was on route from New York to Liverpool, 240 miles east of St. Johns N.F., struck a large iceberg causing her bows to be crushed 20 feet. There was no leakage beyond the forward collision bulkhead. She headed to St John's for repair, during which time it was reported that 200 tons of compressed ice, which was packed tight into the bow section, had to be painstakingly removed before repairs could be undertaken. According to reports, her arrival created a sensation, and hundreds of people visited her at Shea's wharf while she waited for repairs. There she was fitted with a temporary bow made of wood to permit her to sail for Glasgow, where her original builders on the Clyde fitted a new bow.

(norwayheritage.com)

Oscar Wilde said of his trip on board the *Arizona* in January 1882;

> "I was very much disappointed in the Atlantic Ocean. It was very tame. I expected to have it roar about and be beautiful in its storms. I was disappointed in it."
> (Oscar Wilde Quotes. http://www.oscarwildeinamerica.org/quotations/)

Had he been a passenger on the *Arizona* that November in 1879, he might have a livelier voyage on which to make a comment. His facile remarks demeaned the very real dangers and disrespected those who had perished on similar ocean passages previously.
(https://archive.org/details/18820103newyorksunoscarwildeinnewyork)

The decade commencing 1881 recorded an increase in vessels colliding with icebergs; the number of lives lost was 93. Undoubtedly, the most intriguing report was that of the 1705grt British cargo vessel *Resolven* built by Palmer's yard on the Tyne in 1882, which was found adrift off Catalina by H.M.S. *Mallard* in August 1884 and towed to the nearest port. No trace of her was ever found of her crew of seven and four passengers.

It is possible that the crew may have panicked when the ship was damaged by ice and launched the lifeboat, which was then swamped in the panic. No bodies were ever found. The mystery of this ship earned it the nickname, "The Welsh Mary Celeste" after the American merchant sailing vessel of the same name was discovered adrift and abandoned off the Azores on December 4, 1872.

Three years later, the *Resolven* was wrecked while returning to Newfoundland from Nova Scotia with a load of timber.

The Newfoundland sealer *Young Prince* collided with an iceberg in the Gulf of St. Lawrence and sank almost immediately on April 19, 1885. Her crew of 32 made it onto an ice floe, where they remained for 19 days before being rescued by the *Etoile Des Mers*.
(www.wrecksite.eu)

On May 21, 1882, the New York Times reported the six surviving crew members of the *Western Belle*, which struck an iceberg and sank soon after, were brought into port by the schooner *President*. The captain and 13 members of the crew lost their lives when the lifeboat overturned as the vessel went down.
(New York Times, May 21, 1882)

On November 28, 1890, the 3032grt *Thanemore* left Baltimore for London with 38 crew, ten cattlemen and 430 head of cattle and general cargo. It is presumed that she struck an iceberg and sank with the loss of all on board.
(www.wrecksite.eu)

The remaining 11 additional lives were lost in four other incidents.

The years 1901-1912 to the period before the loss of the *Titanic* saw 57 incidents where collisions with ice resulted in the death of about 20 in 5 separate incidents. Additionally, apart from the *Titanic*, the greatest loss of life during this period occurred with the sinking of the Canadian Pacific vessel *Islander* which struck an iceberg and foundered shortly after, taking the lives of up to 65 passengers and crew, including the captain. The remaining 107 were able to reach safety.

In April 1912, passengers and crew of the *Corsican* suffered a scare after crashing into the same field of ice the *Titanic* encountered. The captain immediately gave orders for the vessel to slow down, and steaming less than five knots an hour, the *Corsican* picked its way through the ice, reaching St. John's with all safe on board. They wired a message about the ice to the *Corinthian*, who, it is supposed, passed it on to the *Titanic*. The *Titanic*, we know, likely came across the same ice field a few days later.

There were other incidents:

The 4329grt S.S. *Iowa* was a British iron-hulled passenger/cargo vessel that was on route from Boston to Liverpool carrying passengers & general cargo when she foundered in ice on February 22, 1891. She was owned from 1882 by the Iowa S.S. Co Ltd, Liverpool, England.
(Lloyd's Register of Casualty Returns)

On February 21, 1883, British freighter S.S. *Gloucester City* collided with an iceberg and sank. She was en route from Bristol to New York with general cargo.
(Dictionary of Disasters at Sea During the Age of Steam: 1824-1962, Vol 1 A-L. Charles Hocking, 1969)

The Allan Lines SS *Canadian* was returning to Liverpool with passengers and mail under the command of Capt. Graham. On June 4, 1861, when in the Straits of Belle Isle, the vessel ran into ice and was holed about 10 miles from shore. The damage was fatal, and half an hour later, the *Canadian* sank. Most of the passengers were taken off in safety by the ship's boats, but one of these capsized, drowning 35 people.
(Dictionary of Disasters at Sea During the Age of Steam: 1824-1962, Vol 1 A-L. Charles Hocking, 1969)

Mentioned earlier, and included in the Board of Trade tables was the Dominion Lines S.S. *Vicksburg*, which, on

what was to be her final voyage on April 28, 1875, on route from Liverpool to Quebec, sank following a collision with an iceberg near Newfoundland with the loss of 47 lives. Seven of the crew of the *Vicksburg* were picked up in a nearly exhausted condition by a steamer bound to New York, and two other boats were picked up, containing more of the crew and only three of the passengers.
(New York Times, June 11, 1875)

The S.S. *Merrimac* was a British ocean liner built in 1890 by Harland & Wolfe for the Elder Dempster Line. On October 25, 1899, *Merrimac* set sail from Quebec for Belfast but was never seen again. She was presumed lost to an iceberg. Her crew of 36 perished with the ship.

Returning to the British Inquiry and showing the determination for which, he was renowned, Mr Cotter was not ready to concede;

> "There is one case, if I may bring it to your Lordship's notice. The White Star Line steamer "Naronic" left Liverpool in 1893 and was never heard of again. All her crew went down with her."

Recognising that Cotter had exposed a pertinent point that challenged Sir Robert Finlay's argument, the Commissioner asked;

> "Yes, but do we know anything about the cause of the wreck?"

Almost in desperation, Sir Robert Finlay interrupted and added:

> "No, it may have been a derelict, or anything, or a leak. She was not a passenger ship."

A dismissive response, revealing the attitude of the White Star counsel and officials towards its officers and crew and another reason why there was growing unrest in the shipping industry and the inexorable movement towards the organisation of trades union representation and the deep-seated resentment towards ship owners with the treatment of crewmen aboard their vessels. Sir Robert Finlay's attempts at a vague dismissal of the cause of the loss; "*it may have been a derelict, or anything, or a leak,*" belied White Star's own propensity for encouraging favourable publicity when they lavishly describe to the Press their vessels qualities.

"The "Naronic" is a twin-screw steamship of very recent construction, fitted with all modern appliances. Her machinery may have become disabled, but as she is fitted with a duplicate set of engines, it is not likely that both have become unserviceable. The breaking of her rudder would not seriously interfere with her progress, as she would have a means of steering in her twin propellors. Her numerous bulkheads would seem to insure flotation in case of collision, and she is constructed of steel there does not seem much to fear from fire."

(New York Times, March 2, 1893)

Findlay's pitiful attempts to dismiss the loss as anything other than an iceberg is shameful and desperate. The following day while concern was growing regarding her non-appearance another explanation was suggested;

> "Being schooner rigged, her sail power is very small, but under favorable circumstances it is calculated that she could accomplish about fifty miles a day."

(New York Times, March 3, 1893)

However, by March 21, hope was all but gone. Another report in the New York Times brought news of the discovery by the British steamer *Coventry*, of an overturned lifeboat, painted white, bearing the name *Naronic*. Later the same day, another lifeboat, adrift, also from the *Naronic* was passed. This time, there was indications that this boat had encountered heavy weather. Further on the same article went on to state;

> "It may be, judging from the latitude and longitude in which the boats were seen, that the steamer struck either a derelict or an iceberg, though it is still rather early in the season for ice to be adrift so far south as the Banks."

(New York Times, March 21, 1893)

Lord Mersey failed to pursue the question any further, perhaps sensing he could stray into territory that he thought wiser to avoid. Some months after her disappearance, when it was realised that it was unlikely to find the *Naronic* adrift at sea, in June 1893, a Commission of Inquiry was convened at the initiative of the Board of Trade in Liverpool to establish what few facts were known and to allay the rumour and speculation that had been circulating since the vessel became overdue with 77 souls unaccounted for. Despite Finlay's strenuous exertions to belittle the *Naronic* in the eyes of the Court, "*she was not a passenger ship*," that figure, is further broken down in the

Board of Trade's own records produced for the Inquiry (p330) listed under 'missing' showing *Naronic* as carrying 74 crew, including 17 cattlemen on articles, and 3 passengers. How this 'oversight' was excluded from any conversation during this phase of the Inquiry is suspicious. White Star ardently refuted any claims that *Naronic* had struck an iceberg; however, in the absence of any other substantive evidence to the contrary, that remained the most likely possibility.

(Department Paper 250 p303-31MT9/920F)

In his last sentence, Sir Robert was correct; *Naronic* was not a passenger vessel; the ship had been built as a vessel to transport livestock, mainly cattle, with passenger accommodations added to allow White Star to compete for additional revenue on East Coast routes. There was no chance Finlay would countenance an admission that vessels other than passenger ships could encounter icebergs and come off worse, endangering all on board, from barques and schooners among the numbers, as well as sealers, whalers, and trawlers to larger cargo vessels.

As mentioned previously, in circumstances very similar to that of *Naronic*, in February 1902, on a voyage from Glasgow to St John's N.B., the independent Allen Lines vessel S.S. *Huronian* was reported missing with 57 onboard, including one passenger. Despite extensive searches for many weeks, she was never found. Except, as far as Harold Sanderson and Sir Robert Finlay were concerned, these events seemingly did not count, it was not a White Star vessel. However, the incident did occur somewhere in the

North Atlantic, possibly the same stretch of ocean that in ten years would become *Titanic*'s final resting place.

In the decade before the *Titanic* disaster, reports indicate just over 50 incidents involving collisions with ice, occurring in the same area with varying degrees of damage and disability to the vessel, many serious enough to terminate the planned voyage to seek essential repairs.

Mentioned in Sir Walter Howells tables of vessels lost with over 50 souls was the S.S. *Humber*, conveniently overlooked by the Court when in fact the Official Inquiry into her loss (No 2644) determined in August 1885, six months after she went missing, that she had a crew of 65 hands, not the 55 listed in the Board of Trade Tables provided for the British Inquiry. The Inquiry presided over by Wreck Commissioner H.C. Rothery stated;

> "The Court, having carefully inquired into the circumstances of the above-mentioned shipping casualty, finds, for the reasons annexed, that the vessel when she left New York was very deeply laden, and that her loss was probably due either to her having foundered in the gale which soon afterwards sprang up, or to her having become embedded in the ice which was floating about in the North Atlantic across the track which she would probably take."

She was built on the Clyde at Govan for the Shire Line, in 1880 and named S.S. *Montgomeryshire* before being acquired by the Royal Mail Lines and, fatefully as it transpired, renamed Humber.

(Wrecksite - Humber Cargo Ship 1880-1885)

On the same table, the Anchor Lines, SS *Ismailia* is also listed as "missing" with a crew of 42 and 8 passengers and although there was little to go on the New York World wrote enigmatically.

> "Weather and wind are very changeable at this season of the year, she may have met with further obstacles in reaching port."

(Wrecksite - Ismailia Passenger/Cargo Ship 1870-1873)

The very same week *Titanic* foundered, another documented case was that of S.S. *Niagara*, on April 17, 1912, near the location where *Titanic* had gone down, while negotiating an ice field in dense fog, collided with a large piece of ice with such force the captain sent out an SOS before an inspection revealed no serious damage had occurred and he was able to reassure the startled passengers. He then wired a second cable to confirm he would continue his voyage to New York unassisted. At about the same time, another liner, the *Tunisian*, met a similar fate en route from Liverpool to Montreal, which left her with serious water ingress after a collision off Cape Race. As mentioned previously, in yet another newspaper report, on July 11, just over a week after the *Titanic* Inquiry concluded, the North German Lloyd passenger liner *Kron Prinz Wilhelm*, with 1,172 passengers, also narrowly avoided a serious collision with an iceberg when off the Grand Banks she spotted an iceberg ahead and took avoiding action. The vessel was travelling at about 16 knots at the time and still made contact sufficient to cause large amounts of ice to break off and scrape paint off the side of the ship. The iceberg was stated to be about 50 feet above

the waterline and of a pyramid shape. From the details in the report, there was violent contact made, and it was largely due to the vessel's reduced speed that a more serious incident was avoided.
(New York Times, April 16, 1912)

One can hope that the sage words of Professor Biles would be heard around the Scottish Drill Hall when he was invited to become one of the Assessors appointed by the Home Office to attend the British Inquiry and hopefully provide wise counsel when decisions were being made.

> "Against an indefinite, unknown and unpredictable damage, which a collision with an iceberg could cause, the provision has been insufficient. To renew our vigilance, we must consider the question of safety of ships from the point of view of this contingency."

(The Loss Of The Titanic. By Professor J. H. Biles. The Engineer. April 19, 1912, page 409)

Together, these incidents with large passenger-carrying vessels had a common theme, where more serious damage was negated by the enforced reduction of speed when they were in conditions of reduced visibility, in two cases, dense fog. Sir Robert Finlay's insistence on focusing purely on the *Titanic* ignored many other cases where not only ice was a causative factor and was dismissing other potentially disastrous calamities.

Almost one year before the *Titanic* foundered on April 4, 1911, the North German Lloyd steamship *Prinzess Irene* ran aground off Fire Island parallel to the south shore of Long Island, New York, with 2,100 passengers remaining stuck on a sandbar for four days in rough seas while her passengers were transferred in lifeboats to her sister ship *Prinz Friederich Wilhelm*. The transfer of her passengers by lifeboat took just over five hours.

(New York Times, July 11, 1912)

Sir Robert Finlay's assertions that there were few incidents involving ice which had resulted in loss of life were technically correct, but to suggest that there were only ever a few incidents could be compared with the theological metaphor of counting "*angels dancing on the head of a pin*" which could be identified with White Star counsel's assertions that only incidents which resulted in the loss of life to first-class passengers counted.

The phrase 'it's an ill wind that blows nobody any good' had a certain resonance during the spring period of 1909, when it was reported that at least ten passenger vessels sought refuge and essential repairs in the repair yards of St John's N.F. and Sydney N.B. During the winter season, the repair yards were used to vessels coming into port with damage to their structure from collisions with ice. The local economy prospered due to the vagaries of nature and the impetuosity of ship captains. Latterly, the International Ice Patrol published a list of ships known to have struck icebergs. In that list, there are many examples of ships that struck icebergs head-on and suffered major damage, particularly to the bow section, usually resulting in an aborted voyage, the main collision bulkhead holding, and the ship made her way, even sometimes by backing-up, safely into port for essential repairs. In other cases, the vessel was written off or lost. The year before *Titanic*, it was reported that the Anchor Lines S.S. *Columbia* had her bows damaged by a collision with an iceberg in 'intermittent' fog. The New York Sun reported the incident as her bows being forced back as far as her collision bulkhead, which although leaking, held until she made port for repairs.

(Liner Hits Iceberg, Twisting Her Bow. New York Times, August 5, 1911)

Two years before that, the S.S. *Regulus* suffered extensive damage to the bow plates, variously reported as the worst seen in St. John's in decades, and the vessel remained afloat.

(Historical record of sea ice and iceberg distribution around Newfoundland and Labrador 1810-1958. National Research Council Canada. Hill, B. 7th International Conference and Exhibition on Performance of Ships and Structures in Ice, July 16-19, 2006, Banff, Alberta, Canada, Publication date: 2006.)
(Ship collision with iceberg database www.icedata.ca/)

That Sir Robert Finlay could weave such a tapestry of desperation in his pleadings that icebergs were a rare commodity in the North Atlantic is somewhat repudiated by an article which appeared in the New York Times only a few days after the sinking of the *Titanic*;

> "Of all the terrors of the sea, none is more terrible than the iceberg. Floating from the mysterious North, these colossal ice giants blunder over the seas, and woe to the ship that happens across their course. Worse than fogs, worse than the dreaded derelicts, icebergs have long occupied first place among the perils of the deep in the minds of mariners who must venture over a northerly lane at the seasons when they are rife. What the terrible possibilities of these icy mountains are, was amply proved last week when the Titanic, the biggest ship ever made by man, drove into one of them and was hurled, torn asunder, to the bottom of the ocean."

(Mystery, Tragedy, and Adventure in Icebergs Path. New York Times, April 21, 1912)

The article went on to mention other historical shipping incidents where ice was a factor: the passenger steamship, S.S. *City of Glasgow* mentioned previously, of the Inman Line disappeared en route from Liverpool to Philadelphia in March 1854 with 480 passengers and crew. Her sister ship, the *City of Manchester*, arriving at Liverpool on March 17, reported that there was a large field of broken ice drifting on the course taken by the mail steamships. During her short career, the *City of Glasgow* was to prove that screw propulsion was reliable and superior to paddle wheels, which struggled to make headway in rough seas. Conditions on board for emigrants were significantly improved following a refit in 1852 when she became the first Atlantic steamship to carry steerage passengers.

(Dictionary of Disasters at Sea During the Age of Steam: 1824-1962, Vol 1 A-L. Charles Hocking, 1969)

In yet another report, one newspaper account said;
Shipping Disasters in the Atlantic

> "Vessels arriving here bring accounts of icebergs having been encountered in their passage across the Atlantic. On the 2nd inst. The Notting Hill, a nearly new steel steamship of four thousand tons burthen, the first twin-screw propelled steamer in Trans-Atlantic trade, which was on a voyage hither from London, fell in with ice about midnight. Although she was going dead slow at the time, an iceberg struck her on the port side, rebounded, and struck her again. It made two holes in the vessel's side, near the engine room; the water rushed in a put the

fires out. The Notting Hill drifted for three days when the steamer State of Nebraska fell in with her and rescued all hands."

(wrecksite.eu)
(TheShipsList: Passengers, Ships, Shipwrecks)

Sir Robert Finlay had no basis on which to claim collisions with icebergs were a rare event. The risk was confined to only a few months each year. The history of navigation in the decades leading up to the turn of the 20th century records an extensive number of casualties that occurred in the vicinity of the Grand Banks. Between 1882 and 1890, 14 vessels were lost, and 40 were seriously damaged due to ice. This figure does not take into account a number of whaling, sealers, and fishing vessels also lost or damaged by ice.

In a magazine article, renowned U.S. Navy architect D. W. Taylor, U.S.N., regarded as one of the foremost authorities on ship construction, opened by stating;

"The "Titanic" catastrophe teaches no new lesson as regards the fallibility of man. It simply furnished another example of the well-established principle that if in the conduct of any enterprise, an error of human judgment or faulty working of the human senses involves disaster, sooner or later the disaster comes."

(D.W. Taylor, "Lessons from "Titanic" Disaster" in Popular Mechanics Magazine, Vol. 17, No. 6, June 1912, p. 797-808)

Damage to vessels from ice was not confined to collisions with icebergs. An 1899 newspaper report gave an account of the dangers involved when ice forms on the deck of a ship during a winter storm at sea.

(New York Times, February 12, 1899)
In this story, it was reported that during a period of severe weather, a German vessel, the *Fuerst Bismark*, of the Hamburg-American Line ploughed a furrow through New York harbour ice to reach port finally;

> "As she came up the bay, she presented an unusually brilliant spectacle. Her hull was armoured in ice: Bulwarks and rails were swollen to an abnormal thickness, her bridge rigging, and top hamper generally were massive in frozen spray, and although only ice encased her, it was so white that she looked as though a heavy clinging snow had fallen upon her."

This was accentuated when the same report told of the White Star vessel *Germanic*, which limped into port, and she too was coated in ice and; "*looked like a visitor from the arctic regions,*" with an estimated 500 tons of ice all about her and noticeably listing to starboard, made unstable with the additional, weight. The *Germanic's* ordeal did not end there. Two days later, with much of the ice remaining, while still tied up at Pier 45, she became top-heavy when her cargo was removed. The report continued;

> "While the ship was being coaled an unfortunate accident occurred. Most of the coal was on the port or north side, making the ship list to that side. The report describes. The heavy wind and the roughness of the river, together with the untrimmed cargo of coal and the weight of ice high above the centre of gravity, made the ship very unstable and she rocked greatly. A small hurricane

struck the river at 9:30 o'clock causing the vessel to roll away over to port, submerging the open coal holes, and permitting her to ship a great quantity of water into her bunkers."

Over the next few days, there were daily reports on the progress. As enthralled New Yorkers looked on, the New York Times reported over the following days: The *Germanic* lay ignominiously in her berth at the White Star Line pier, resting easily on an even keel on the mud. Her hold was flooded, and divers were at work closing the bunker ports, through which the water that sank her on Monday night had flowed.

(New York Times, February 14, 1899)

As a consequence of the acquisition in 1902 of the Dominion Line by the International Mercantile Marine Co., in 1908, a joint service was operated with both White Star and Dominion Lines vessels to and from Montreal in Canada, which operated under the banner "White Star-Dominion Line." This explains why the *Teutonic* found herself steaming in heavy fog on the return trip from Montreal to Liverpool and had a heart-stopping brush with disaster when at about 3 30pm on October 22, 1913, operating under this shared agreement, she encountered an iceberg off Belle Isle, 172 miles east of Newfoundland.

Unlike the *Titanic*, almost eighteen months previously, on this occasion, fortune was on the side of the White Star liner. According to reports, as a jagged outline emerged out of the fog, a lookout posted on the forecastle alerted the captain, who immediately ordered the helm hard to port and the engines thrown into full reverse, a chilling replay similar to the actions taken on the bridge of the *Titanic* on her fateful night. According to eyewitnesses, the iceberg glided by the vessel less than 20 feet away. *Teutonic* sailed on unscathed.

One dramatic headline read; "Teutonic Menaced by Giant Iceberg."
(New York Times. October 28, 1913)

Whereas, the Chicago Tribune reported;

Just Missed Titanic's Fate

"The fog was so thick that even at that small distance the berg could scarcely be distinguished. It was so close that there was danger that the propeller of the ship would strike it as the vessel went around."
(Tuesday, October 28, 1913)

In an editorial in the Daily Mail, before confirmation of the sinking of the *Titanic* and the resulting loss of life reached these shores, the widely held views of so many were about to be brutally exposed. The fixation in the minds of the shipping industry and the public in general that modern technology and sheer size implied greater strength was incited by an enthusiastic press:

The Accident To The Titanic

> "Seldom indeed has a more thrilling tale been told to the people of two continents than that of the strange incident to the White Star liner Titanic, which all day and night was coming in by instalments, as the wireless messages sped over the waters of the Atlantic from the stricken ship and the vessels which she had called up to her rescue. Their

alternate burden of dismay and hope held the world in suspense.

That so vast and splendid a liner should be in mortal peril verged on the incredible. For the Titanic is a marvel in herself. With her sister, the Olympic, she is the largest ship in the world and the most luxuriously appointed. She carried on her maiden voyage the population of a small town. She was fitted with every device that the wit of man can provide to tame the treachery of the sea. The most perfect system of subdivision, the finest mechanical contrivances of the engineer, all were embodied in her design. Yet this wonder among vessels of the world has all but succumbed to one of the most familiar if most insidious of ocean perils. On Sunday night she struck an iceberg with such terrific violence that those in charge of her evidently feared her immediate loss."

The article went on;

"A smaller ship than the Titanic might well have succumbed to the concussion caused by striking this stupendous field of ice. The question is often asked whether the size of our modern ships is a real gain. This incident supplies the answer. The Titanic escaped without, so far as we know, any loss of life. She is still afloat and there is a fair chance of her reaching a port if the weather holds good. A ship of her dimensions, measuring 850 ft. in length, with a displacement of water of 50,000 tons, is for all practical purposes unsinkable. Her bulk is a protection, not a danger. The most violent collision means the crumpling up of her bows, at the worst, and the filling of her forward compartments. But with her gigantic size and the system by which every watertight door in her bulkheads can be closed from the bridge, she can still float and even steam after such a disaster. Modern methods of ship construction have been put to the most crucial test that can possible be imagined, and they have triumphed. The affair of the Titanic is a fresh proof of the safety of the modern steam vessel, a fresh illustration of the dominance which man has established over the most treacherous forces of nature."

(Daily Mail, Tuesday, April 16, 1912)

The days and weeks that followed would reveal the true extent of the regulatory failures and false promises of shipbuilders and politicians over many years to enact the most prudent of measures to ensure the safety of vessels at sea.

The dishonest representation made by civil servants whose job it was to secure the safest means of crossing the world's oceans, were, in the end only ever about preserving reputations and the pursuit of profit.

Epilogue

German philosopher Friedrich Nietzsche did not survive the first year of the 20th century. However, his prescient musings have been discussed and debated ever since. One of his many quotations, "*They muddy the water, to make it seem*

deep," is a fitting synopsis of Sir Robert Finlay and his counsel defending the White Star Line and Captain Smith.
(Friedrich Wilhelm Nietzsche, Thus Spoke Zarathustra A Book for All and None)

His obfuscations and promptings of evidence and witnesses to make their testimony appear more substantial than it was beguiled the court and created enough ambiguity for Lord Mersey to arrive at his conclusions despite rather than in favour of the truth.

Fin

About The Author

Ian Donaldson has a professional background in clinical research and health care education spanning over thirty years. He is married with grown up children and lives in the Scottish Highlands where he enjoys his leisure time playing piano and walking his dogs.

titanicthetruthontrial@gmail.com

Bibliography

Official Publications

Report of a Formal Investigation into the circumstances attending the foundering on 15th April 1912, of the British steamship "Titanic," of Liverpool, after striking ice in or near Latitude 41° 46' N., Longitude 50° 14' W, North Atlantic Ocean, whereby loss of life ensued London: HMSO, Cd 6352

LORD MERSEY'S REPORT. HC Deb 07 October 1912 vol 42 cc32-148

BOARD OF TRADE—LOSS OF LIFE AT SEA. HC Deb 21 May 1912 vol 38 cc1757-829

US Congress, Senate, Report of the Senate Committee on Commerce pursuant to S. Res. 283, Directing the Committee to Investigate the Causes of the Sinking of the 'Titanic', with speeches by William Alden Smith and Isidor Rayner, 62d Cong., 2d sess., 28 May 1912, S. Rept. 806 (6127), Washington, Government Printing Office

Online Resources

Lloyd's Register of Shipping | The National Archives

Lloyd's Register Casualty Returns : Lloyd's Register Foundation:

Casualty Returns (lrfoundation.org.uk)

www.wikipedia.org

www.Titanicinquiry.org

www.wrecksite.eu

www.theshipslist.com

www.norwayheritage.com

www.encyclopedia-Titanica.org

www.ukwhoswho.com

www.paperlessarchives.com

hansard.parliament.uk

www.nationalarchives.gov.uk

www.nytimes.com

www.newspapers.com

www.thetimes.co.uk

www.gracesguide.co.uk

www.dailymail.co.uk

N.B. Some of the above may require a donation, subscription, or purchase.

Books and Journals

The Loss of the SS Titanic Lawrence Beesley June 1912

"Titanic": A Survivor's Story. Colonel Archibald Gracie 1913

Comdr. Lightoller, 'Titanic' and other ships (London: I. Nicholson and Watson, 1935)

Report On The Loss Of The S.S. Titanic. Sutton Publishing 1990

The Titanic Disaster Hearings: The Official Transcripts of the 1912 Senate Investigation, edited by Tom Kuntz (New York: Pocket Books, 1998).

Dictionary of Disasters at Sea During the Age of Steam: Including Sailing Ships and Ships of War Lost in Action, 1824-1962, Volume I&II Charles Hocking, 1969

Department of Transport, Marine Accident Investigation Branch, RMS "Titanic": Reappraisal of evidence relating to SS "Californian" (London: HMSO, 1992)

The 'Deathless Story of the Titanic' Philip Gibbs, Lloyd's Weekly News, April 1912.

Sealed Orders, Helen Churchill Candee. Originally published in Collier's Weekly, 4 May 1912

Sea-Toll of our Time. R.L. Hadfield. The Nautilus Library. 1935

Notes on Life and Letters Joseph Conrad SOME REFLECTIONS ON THE LOSS OF THE TITANIC – 1912. p213-228. DoubleDay, Page & Company 1921

Atlantic Conquest, Warren Tute, Cassell 1962

The Plimsoll Line, George Peters, Barry Rose (Publishers) 1975.)

North Atlantic Seaway Vol 2 N.R.P. Bonsor, Brookside Publishers 1978

Great Passenger Ships Of The World Volume 1 1858-1912 Arnold Kludas 1975

Ships of the World An Historical Encyclopedia Lincoln Paine. 1995

00000

Index

The Attorney-General, 8, 13, 15, 59, 62, 63, 64, 65, 67, 68, 69, 71, 82, 83, 84, 85, 86, 92, 93, 94, 95, 96, 97, 101, 104, 112, 115, 116, 117, 119, 120, 127, 132, 134, 145, 146, 147, 148, 149, 150, 151, 152, 153, 155, 159, 186, 187, 194, 201, 202, 203, 205, 206

Board of Trade, 6, 8, 14, 15, 16, 57, 59, 60, 61, 62, 70, 71, 72, 73, 75, 76, 77, 78, 80, 81, 82, 84, 86, 87, 88, 92, 93, 94, 96, 97, 100, 101, 102, 103, 104, 105, 106, 107, 108, 109, 110, 111, 112, 113, 114, 116, 119, 120, 122, 123, 124, 126, 127, 129, 131, 132, 133, 136, 137, 139, 140, 141, 143, 145, 146, 148, 149, 150, 151, 152, 153, 154, 155, 159, 160, 161, 165, 166, 168, 170, 173, 174, 179, 180, 181, 182, 183, 188, 189, 198, 199, 203, 213, 216, 217

Mr Butler Aspinall, 128, 141

Captain Smith, 33, 36, 70, 138, 166, 183, 191, 194, 229

Charles Lightoller, 39

Harold Sanderson, 11, 12, 14, 15, 17, 20, 24, 30, 31, 32, 60, 74, 149, 150, 182, 217

Havelock Wilson, 77

J. Bruce Ismay, 36

J.P. Morgan, 20, 26

Lord Mersey, 5, 7, 9, 11, 38, 54, 58, 59, 60, 61, 67, 70, 84, 92, 93, 97, 110, 111, 112, 117, 118, 119, 120, 121, 123, 124, 125, 126, 129, 132, 134, 135, 136, 137, 138, 139, 140, 141, 143, 144, 145, 146, 147, 149, 151, 160, 161, 162, 163, 164, 165, 166, 167, 168, 169, 179, 181, 186, 187, 190, 192, 193, 194, 195, 200, 202, 203, 204, 216, 229

Lord Muskerry, 105, 107, 108, 109, 110

Mr Buxton, 139, 169, 170, 198, 199

Mr Edwards, 122, 123, 124

Mr Scanlan, 121, 122, 133, 134

Philip Franklin, 18, 20

President of the Board of Trade, 16, 55, 75, 76, 78, 110, 111, 139, 162, 169, 171, 172, 198, 199

Sir Alfred Chalmers, 98, 120, 121, 150, 159, 160, 161

Sir Norman Hill, 59, 85, 127, 129, 130, 131, 133, 134, 135, 138, 141, 142, 143, 153, 155, 158, 164, 180

Sir Robert Finlay, 11, 12, 13, 14, 15, 17, 26, 27, 31, 32, 57, 75, 127, 151, 153, 165, 166, 167, 179, 180, 181, 182, 184, 185, 186, 187, 189, 190, 191, 192, 193, 194, 196, 200, 201, 202, 203, 204, 205, 207, 214, 217, 220, 221, 223, 229

Sir Rufus Isaacs, 8, 64, 71, 83, 97, 101, 134, 146, 148, 181, 194, 203, 205, 206

Sir Walter Howell, 54, 59, 61, 64, 68, 70, 71, 72, 83, 84, 85, 92, 94, 96, 97, 105, 109, 110, 111, 112, 113, 115, 117, 118, 120, 121, 125, 126, 127, 138, 143, 146, 151, 155, 156, 159, 164, 166, 173

Stanley Lord, 95, 102

Sydney Buxton, 108, 140, 162, 163, 168, 171, 173, 198

Thomas Ismay, 38, 42, 58

White Star Line, 9, 11, 12, 14, 15, 18, 24, 26, 27, 30, 31, 32, 33, 35, 36, 37, 38, 39, 45, 46, 51, 53, 60, 71, 75, 85, 105, 148, 149, 152, 180, 182, 192, 195, 200, 203, 206, 207, 214, 225, 229

Winston Churchill, 15, 16, 162

Printed in Great Britain
by Amazon